AMERICA PERCEIVED:

A View from Abroad
in the 20th Century

AMERICA PERCEIVED

¤ America Perceived: A View From Abroad
in the 17th Century

¤ America Perceived: A View From Abroad
in the 18th Century

¤ America Perceived: A View From Abroad
in the 19th Century

✖ America Perceived: A View From Abroad
in the 20th Century

AMERICA PERCEIVED:

A View from Abroad in the 20th Century

Edited by
Orm Överland

Series Editor
James Axtell

Pendulum Press, Inc.

West Haven, Connecticut   El Monte, California

Clothbound Edition   *ISBN 0-88301-144-1*   *Complete Set*
                          0-88301-148-4   *This Volume*

Paperback Edition   *ISBN 0-88301-123-9*   *Complete Set*
                          0-88301-127-1   *This Volume*

Library of Congress Catalog Card Number   73-94110

JUL 2 '74

Published by
Pendulum Press, Inc.
An Academic Industries, Inc. Company
The Academic Building
Saw Mill Road
West Haven, Connecticut 06516

Printed in the United States of America

CONTENTS

ABOUT THE EDITOR

Orm Överland, Associate Professor at the University of Bergen, Norway, received his bachelor's and master's degrees from the University of Oslo. He later received a Ph.D. in American Studies from Yale University. He is the recipient of three fellowships: the Haakon VII Fellowship from Norway-America Association, an American Studies Fellowship from American Council of Learned Societies, and a Research Fellowship from the University of Oslo. Mr. Överland has written several articles in both European and American journals, and is the editor of *American Studies in Scandinavia*.

ABOUT THE SERIES EDITOR

James Axtell, after receiving his B.A. from Yale University, went on to study at Oxford International Summer School, and later received his Ph.D. from Cambridge University. Mr. Axtell has taught at Yale University and currently is Associate Professor of history at Sarah Lawrence College. He has published many articles, reviews, and essays and has served as general editor of several educational publications. He is the author of the forthcoming book, *The School upon a Hill: Education and Society in Colonial New England*.

FOREWORD

> Oh wad some power the giftie gie us
> To see ourselves as others see us!
> It wad frae monie a blunder free us,
>   An' foolish notion.
>   Robert Burns, "To a Louse" (1786)

AMERICA PERCEIVED was created as a companion to THE AMERICAN PEOPLE series and as an independent collection of primary sources for the study of American history. Like its companion, it is founded on the belief that the study of history in the schools and junior levels of college generally begins at the wrong end. That study usually begins with abstract and pre-digested *conclusions*—the conclusions of other historians as filtered through the pen of a textbook writer—and not with the primary sources of the past and unanswered *questions* —the starting place of the historian himself.

Since we all need, use, and think about the past in our daily lives, we are all historians. The question is whether we can be skillful, accurate, and useful historians. The only way to become such is to exercise our historical skills and interests until we gain competence. But we have to exercise them in the same ways the best historians do or we will be kidding ourselves that we are *doing* history when in fact we are only absorbing sponge-like the results of someone else's historical competence.

Historical competence must begin with one crucial skill—the ability to distinguish between past and present. Without a sharp sense of the past as a different time from our own, we will be unable to accord the people of the past the respect that we would like to receive from

7

the people of the future. And without according them that respect, we will be unable to recognize their integrity as individuals or to understand them as human beings like ourselves.

A good sense of the past depends primarily on a good sense of the present, on experience, and on the imaginative empathy to relate ourselves to human situations not our own. Since most students have had a relatively brief experience of life and have not yet given full expression to their imaginative sympathies, THE AMERICAN PEOPLE was designed to draw upon the one essential prerequisite for the study of history that all students possess—the lives they have lived from birth to young adulthood. It asked us to look at the American experience from the *inside*, through the eyes of the participants who lived through the American life cycles, with the understanding gained from living through our own. AMERICA PERCEIVED seeks to draw more upon our imaginative sympathy by asking us to look at America from the *outside*, through the eyes of visitors, travellers, and critics whose lives and values were very different from those of the Americans they saw.

One view (inside or outside) is not necessarily better—that is, more accurate, sensitive, objective, complete—than the other. Both views are necessary to take the full measure of the country in all its complexity. The value of the view ultimately depends upon the observer. The quality of a foreigner's observations depends less upon his initial attitude toward America than upon his personal qualities—his objectivity, breadth of vision, accuracy of perception, sensitivity to human character, and tolerance of cultural difference. For example, although a perceptive visitor may come to America expecting the worst, his observations may be of great value because he can accurately see some of the country's dark spots and contradictions that perhaps remain hidden to Americans or to other visitors who come expecting only the best. On the other hand, the observations of an insensitive visitor who comes expecting the best may be of small value because he is too accepting of what well-meaning Americans tell him or because he is unable to see the country's faults and contradictions as well as its more obvious strengths and consistencies.

Foreign observers possess one quality that gives special value to their views of America: their foreignness. They are the products of different cultures which do not share all the assumptions, values, and standards of Americans. They see the world differently than Americans because they have been taught by their culture to see the world differently. In any culture there are aspects of life—they may be good or bad—which for some reason its own members are either unable to see or take so much for granted that they are never mentioned. But few cultures develop exactly the same blind spots about the same aspects of life. Consequently, the visiting members of one culture may be able to see those unrecognized or unmentioned aspects of another culture simply because they are used to seeing them—or not seeing them as the case may be—in their own culture. It is this angle of vision that gives the perceptions of foreigners their primary historical value.

But foreigners' observations usually have one built-in limitation: they are static snapshots of America frozen in time. Because of their relatively short stay, travellers seldom capture a full view of the historical development of the country that made it what it is when they see it. They record only the end product of a long process. Of course curiosity, historical research, and a good interviewing technique can overcome some of this limitation, but they can seldom erase it completely. Consequently, to gain an idea of historical change—as well as stability—we must place these snapshots in chronological order and compare them. This is sometimes difficult because travellers may not focus upon comparable subjects in successive periods, but in general the same range of subjects will capture visitors' interest, especially in a period of moderate or slow change. Visitors are adept at avoiding fads.

Since the experience of each student is the only prerequisite for the study of primary sources at the first level, annotations and introductory material have been reduced to a minimum, simply enough to identify the sources, their authors, and the circumstances in which they were written.

But the remains of the past are mute by themselves. Many sources have survived that can tell us what happened in the past and why, but they have to be questioned properly to reveal their secrets. So by way of illustration, a number of questions have been asked in each chapter, but these should be supplemented by the students whose experiences and knowledge and interests are, after all, the flywheel of the educational process. Although the questions and sources are divided into chapters, they should be used freely in the other chapters;

the collection should be treated as a whole. And although most of the illustrative questions are confined to the sources at hand, questions that extend to the present should be asked to anchor the acquired knowledge of the past in the immediate experience of the present. Only then will learning be real and lasting and history brought to life.

INTRODUCTION

The United States continues to fascinate the foreign observer in this century as it did in previous centuries. Indeed, the body of literature by non-Americans on Americans is growing by leaps and bounds. Such growth indicates not only the desire of an increasing number of foreign visitors to communicate their impressions and views but the apparently insatiable appetite of the reading public, in the United States and abroad, for interpretations of American life.

Some of the contributions to this volume resemble that of Georges Duhamel, who claimed he could not "see the Americans for America. . . . . Between the American citizen and me there rises I know not what monstrous phantom, a collection of laws, institutions, prejudices, and even myths, a social machine without an equal in the world, and with no analogue in history. I see a system rather than a people." Others resemble the views of John Buchan, who found that no country could "show such a wide range of type and character, and I am so constituted that in nearly all I find something to interest and attract me." While there are many who offer generalizations about American society, John Buchan also warns against this: "You no sooner construct a rule than it is shattered by the exceptions." Not all observers have been equally aware of the limitations of their own experience of the country.

Their vision is of course colored, but not necessarily obscured, by their own cultural or political prejudices. While none may have told the whole truth about the United States, all these writers have grasped some part of the truth, even though they frequently appear to contradict each other. If the majority of those selected have a critical attitude to many aspects of American society, they are merely following the lead of native writers. Even those who voice extremely negative opinions seem strangely moderate compared with the violent language of their American counterparts.

I. PROLOGUE: WHAT MAKES AN AMERICAN

RAOUL DE ROUSSY DE SALES

Since Hector de Crèvecoeur in 1782 phrased the question: "What then is the American, this new man?" answers have been attempted by succeeding generations of Americans and foreign observers alike. America was an idea before it became a nation and the adjective American has ideological connotations not associated with the corresponding adjectives Belgian, Mongolian or Brasilian. There is no Brasilianism and the Belgians are unaware of any crime called un-Belgianism.

Many observers have tried to define Americanism. For some it is a fascinating concept, for others a menacing one. In 1939 Roussey de Sales (1896-1942), a French journalist who had lived in the United States since 1932, joined the ranks of European commentators who have tried to explain to their hosts their uniqueness. His essay on "What Makes an American" was published in *The Atlantic Monthly* (March 1939), pp. 295-304. Copyright © 1938, ℗ 1966, by the Atlantic Monthly Company, Boston, Mass. Reprinted with permission.

Why is it difficult to coin a satisfactory definition of "American"? Does it stand *for* something or only *against* something? In what sense is America a melting pot of "all creeds" and "all convictions?" In what sense is it not? What part does America's size play in her nationality? What part does attachment to "home" and locality play? What part language? How does American nationality differ from European?

13

It is strange that the only common denominator accepted by all people to-day should be the one which most assuredly prevents them from living in peace with one another. That denominator is nationalism, the strongest single motive which inspires the action of modern men. . . .

To a European, no country is more interesting from this point of view than America, and in the seven years I have lived here none has interested me and puzzled me more.

To begin with, it took me some time to formulate to myself an answer to the very simple questions: 'What makes an American? How does it *feel* to belong to this nation?'

These questions will naturally sound absurd to an American, and he might retort, 'Well, how does it feel to be a Frenchman?' But that is just the point—most Frenchmen can tell you quite clearly what makes them conscious of being French, but I have found it very difficult to obtain from my American friends or from my reading a comprehensive definition of the American nationality.

First of all, it is obvious that the sense of nationality is not less developed in Americans than in any other people. It is quite as real and quite as visible in all its manifestations. But the fact that such expressions as 'Americanism,' the 'American way,' the 'American outlook,' and so forth, have had to be coined seems to indicate that Americans are the first to feel the need of qualifying themselves when they say, 'I am an American.' More than that, the American consciousness gives an impression of growth. It is not static, and one feels that it still contains tremendous possibilities of expression.

For the moment, however, there is a very important trait in the make-up of the American nationality which does not exist, I believe, in any other. And that is the fact that America is a permanent protest against the rest of the world, and particularly against Europe.

This attitude has both historical and psychological reasons. Most Americans believe to-day the following facts concerning their nation: (1) that this continent was peopled by men who rebelled against the tyrannies of Europe; (2) that these men dedicated themselves, from the very beginning, to the purposeful establishment of a kind of freedom that should endure forever; (3) that they succeeded, by a 'revolution,' in breaking away forever from the oppressive domination and the cupidity of European imperialisms; (4) that in establishing a democratic government they determined forever the course of political perfection, and that whoever followed another course was on the road to damnation; (5) that although European nations were becoming progressively harmless in relation to the increasing power and resources of the ever-growing America, they remained a potential danger to the integrity of this great nation on account of their deplorable habit of wandering away from the true path of civilization, which is democracy, the pursuit of material comfort and more happiness for everybody on this earth as soon as possible.

An Englishman may have doubts regarding the British Empire, a Frenchman may be discouraged concerning the future of France. There are Germans who are not sure that they represent a superior race. All of them, however, remain thoroughly English, French, or German in spite of everything. The type of American who does not accept America as it is and has misgivings about it—such as Henry James, Edith Wharton, T. S. Eliot, and some others—belongs to a past generation. To-day one seldom meets an American skeptic, for the reason that nothing is more assuredly un-American than to entertain any doubt concerning the fact that somehow or other this country will come out all right.

There are many who will find such a statement too sweeping, and say, for instance, that President Roosevelt is destroying the national ideal, that he is leading the country to ruin, decadence, anarchy, and so forth. But even those objectors are not skeptical about the future of their country. Even they feel that faith in America is what makes them Americans. All their irritation would be assuaged if Mr. Roosevelt were removed, all their confidence restored. This kind of skepticism is skin-deep. It does not affect the soul of Americanism.

This faith, like all faiths, does not engender a passive attitude towards the rest of the world. Americans are tolerant to all creeds and to all convictions, but few people express their distrust and indignation with more vigor whenever some of *their* beliefs are offended. Few people are more conscious that ideas may be more destructive than guns. And rightly so, because if any unorthodox creed really implanted itself in America—if the day came when an American citizen could really feel that his country was not following the right course and that a change was due—the political disunion thus produced would have unforetold consequences. The one serious crisis of this kind that America has known, the Civil War, showed the frightful results of a real political conflict. It nearly made two nations out of one. But this experiment in dissension seems to have served as a lasting lesson. It is difficult to believe that it would be repeated. Unity on the fundamental principles of politics is indispensable to the life of this country. The presence of even a small minority who would question the validity of Americanism would attack at the very core the concept of American nationality itself.

The crisis that shook Europe in September 1938 once more brought out the fact that 99 per cent of Americans distrust Europe as a whole, and that they *must* distrust it to retain the feeling that they are Americans.

This is no place to discuss the events leading up to or the consequences of the Munich peace, but the experience was conclusive. American opinion saw in all this affair one main point: democracy had lost out in the struggle, and something hostile to America had won.

Does this mean that many Frenchmen and many Englishmen do not feel the same way? Certainly not. But even the most ardent opponents of Mr. Chamberlain and M. Daladier, those who feel most bitterly that democracy and freedom are threatened to-day, do not think that their national integrity—their conception of what is British or French—is involved. Many of them may have become what Mrs. Anne O'Hare McCormick appropriately called 'spiritual refugees' within their own country, but—unpleasant as this change may be—it does not go any further.

Not so with the Americans. Most of them to-day have become isolationists. They despair of Europe and are all the more anxious to protect the Western Hemisphere from the anti-democratic plague that is sweeping the world. And at the bottom of their anxiety to preserve their political institutions, their habits of thought, and their form of civilization, there is more than a prejudice against the revolution brought about by the totalitarian doctrines; there is in the heart of every American the positive fear that his existence, as an American, is endangered.

It may seem presumptuous to say that these two fundamental factors —the permanent protest against Europe, and the faith in one definite outlook on life—are the most important qualifications of an American.

One could argue that Americans have a deep attachment to the section of the map which they occupy, and that they would still love it just as much if Hitlerism or Stalinism became the law of the land. This may be so, but it still has to be proved, because for one hundred and fifty years America has known only one form of government, one philosophy of life, and one aim. The elements which make up an Englishman, a Spaniard, or Dutchman are the same as those that make up an American, but the emphasis is different. For instance, Europeans seem to be more deeply aware of their physical relationship to the place they occupy in the sun than are most Americans.

It may be difficult to make this clear to people who profess such a cult of the home, the home town, or the state from which they have come. But, although this love of the motherland is genuine enough, it always appears to a European somewhat abstract, as if it were an acquired taste. Moreover, it is in constant conflict with another impulse, typically American—the urge to move and detach oneself constantly all through one's life from any definite surroundings.

This nomadic instinct is too well known to be emphasized. It has historical causes: the pioneer spirit; the very size of the country; the fact that means of communication, such as railroads, were available before there really was any place to go to; the urban civilization attaining a tremendous development without any marked transition between the village and the big city, and so forth.

But the relative weakness of the physical love of the Americans for their country shows itself most strikingly in very trivial manifestations, which, I believe, puzzle every European observer.

For instance, to travel in America is a psychological experience which cannot be compared with traveling in any other country. Having visited in the last three years approximately one hundred cities for the purpose of lecturing, I find to-day that I have no memory of more than about ten of them. They are mere names in my notebook connected with a few incidents, but very seldom with any characteristic impression of the places themselves. If I were transported to-day on a magic carpet to most of these towns, I should be at a loss to identify them.

The explanation is obvious: there is more monotony in American towns than in those of Europe. There is also the question of distances.

Landscapes and the general surroundings change very slowly in this huge continent. Someone said that Switzerland would be the largest country on earth if it were not *folded*. America is completely *unfolded*, and gives the impression in some places of being positively stretched out.

The European traveler experiences another strange feeling: that his ignorance of the geography of the country is usually shared by most of his traveling companions, who, moreover, seem to be considerably more indifferent about it than he is himself. This does not mean that the average American one meets in a Pullman lounge does not know where he is, or where he is going. As a matter of fact, he is usually more accurate concerning distances between various points and the time it takes to get from one to the other, either in a train or in a plane, than a Frenchman would be in his own country. But his knowledge is abstract. The railroad timetable and the esoteric map therein seem to give him all the information he requires. What actually *happens* between two given points, what the physical make-up of the land is, interests only a few.

Here again I suppose the question of size intervenes. Human senses cannot focus on a whole continent the way the painters of the Italian Renaissance could depict on one piece of canvas, and with all its details, the whole familiar area around them which was, in fact, their country. The American must be content with a simplified and purely convenient kind of blueprint of the forty-eight states and the broad outlines of endless plains, tremendous mountains, and gigantic rivers. . . .

Nostalgia is not an American feeling. True enough, it has been the luck of Americans never to know all through their history the ordeal of exile from America. At one time or another, practically all nations of Europe have expelled some of their citizens for political or religious reasons, and these unfortunate minorities have known this curious human capacity for longing to 'go back' where they came from. In recent years this form of suffering has been imposed on larger and larger sections of human beings. Americans, luckily for them, have been spared this experience. Nevertheless, some of them have had to live abroad for more or less lengthy periods. During the 1920's, for instance, several thousands were established in Paris, but, although they occasionally yearned for 'home,' this yearning was momentary and generally explainable by some local cause of irritation, such as the difficulty of getting accustomed to French coffee, or the amount of rain which falls in France. . . .

I never saw the American exiles sit, like the Russians, around the equivalent of a samovar—namely, a pot of real American coffee—and indulge in an orgy of misery, with appropriate songs, over the fact that they were so far away from Buffalo or Omaha.

Speaking of songs, it is strange that most of those which express nostalgia come from the Negroes. 'Carry Me Back to Old Virginny' is a good equivalent of the Breton 'J'aime mieux Paimpol et sa falaise,' but it does not express a really American sentiment. As a matter of fact, the number of Americans who want to be 'carried back' to Old Virginia or to any other particular place is remarkably small. When it comes to retiring from active life and dying somewhere, they would rather move to a nice climate, if they can, like California or Florida, than to the place where they were born.

I fear that many readers will object to this statement. They will point out that nowhere in the world is there such a love of the family and of the home as in America. They will show me innumerable proofs that all representative and popular expressions of the American soul—such as the movies and advertising, for instance—play up constantly the theme of the American's love for the old homestead, for the state from which he hails, for his Alma Mater, and so forth. This is true, but I will confess that this concerted effort to boost sentiments which are taken for granted everywhere else gives one an impression of artificiality. The fact that the word 'home,' for instance, can be used and abused to the point of having become meaningless makes one suspect that the millions of people who use it not only do not know what the word really means, but are actually not very much interested in the thing itself.

There are good reasons for this. One is that few Americans live in or near the house where they were born—that is, in their home in the proper sense of the term—because few habitations in America last as long as a man's life. Not infrequently in small towns one sees a single stone building, standing in the midst of less permanent constructions, preserved as a specimen of the home and dedicated to the town as a museum.

Another reason why the home is more a dream than a reality is the survival of early nomadism which in many parts of the country has blended itself with the sense of instability produced by industrialism and purely urban life. All modern countries are following the same trend; everywhere in the world men are returning slowly to the stage of the Bedouin—with complications. Home, for an ever-increasing number of men and women, is simply the place where they find work, and this place changes for most of them with growing rapidity. But in the Old World this trend towards chronic instability is checked by the toughness of the roots which still attach the individual to his province or village.

In France it is rare to find an industrial worker, an employee, or for that matter any *displaced* Frenchman, who has not kept some contact with his relatives who still live in the village or the small town where he himself was born. And it is usually his ambition to go back there when he is old.

Such roots exist in America also, but, with the exception of the oldest states, they are not very deep or very important in a man's life. There is also the tremendous fact that there are no peasants in America—a fact which alone would explain the curious impression that there is some sort of missing link in the structure of American society. 'Peasant' (from the French *paysan*, meaning the man of a *pays*—that is, a very small area which may not encompass more than a village and its surrounding fields) may be a word which sounds badly to American ears, but it nevertheless represents a type of human being whose unchangeability through centuries, and whose total identification with the place where he was born and where he will die, probably constitute the soundest guarantee that some of the strongest virtues and some of the most useful vices of mankind will survive.

There are no American peasants, and this may be the real reason why to so many Americans the love of the land is little more than a poetic expression. It may be the reason why things pertaining to the soil retain a peculiar symbolic quality which is in marked contrast with the poignant connotation that these things have in other countries.

The nearest equivalent to the European peasant is, of course, the farmer, but it is obvious that his outlook on life is more akin to that of the business man than to that of the man who tills the earth. He is already urbanized, and in any event his numbers are rapidly decreasing. Not so very long ago farmers constituted 90 per cent of the population. Now, according to the *Encyclopaedia of the Social Sciences,* they make up only 22 per cent.

In most countries of the Old World, language creates a bond which is often invoked as a proof of national unity. The national language assumes sometimes a character of sacredness. All through the history of Europe, nations have gone to war for the right to speak and write their own language. It would seem a natural human feeling that, when a man loses the privilege of expressing himself in his mother tongue, something fundamental in him has been destroyed. He feels that he can no longer defend himself against an alien culture and an alien domination. And, in fact, history proves that this is very often the case.

French happens to be an extremely difficult language to speak or write correctly, even for a Frenchman, but the French have for their language a veneration which has probably no equivalent anywhere else except perhaps in China, among the mandarins. A man who speaks or writes well enjoys an impressive prestige. No politician can get anywhere in France (even if he represents the most uneducated parts of the country) if his style is not approximately correct. . . .

In America, however, no such importance is attributed to the way a man expresses himself. Nobody requires an orator to speak perfect English. Some do and some don't. But this does not affect their prestige or their power in the least. Indeed, the average American audience has a tendency to resent a speaker whose eloquence is a little too punctilious.

The first reason for this attitude towards the national language is that the American language is still in a vigorous state of creation. It offers vast possibilities of development, and it has already (in my way of thinking) made the kind of English which is spoken and written in England seem as dull and ineffectual as weak tea. Contemporary American writing and the forceful rhythm of good American speech are fast superseding British English. But the whole system of communication used by the Americans between themselves is still as unstable and experimental as was French in the time of Rabelais. And so the American purist has not much chance for another century or two.

Secondly, the language which is supposed to be officially that of the United States cannot be considered with great reverence as long as the millions of non-assimilated or partly assimilated foreign-born or children of foreign-born continue to speak their native tongue. According to statistics, out of 123 million American citizens counted in 1930 there were 53 million divided among the foreign-born and their children. Of course, most of these have learned to speak English, and in doing so have enriched their new language with many words and expressions of their own and even, I believe, with certain intonations and a rhythm which are making the American language what it is. But those who spoke Swedish, Italian, or Polish yesterday cannot be expected to feel that the King's English or General Hugh Johnson's has become part of their blood and that it is an important element in their national consciousness.

A final factor which makes the concept of American nationality so difficult for the foreigner to grasp is the impossibility of giving a unified picture of a nation which does not really occupy a country, but is spread out all over a continent. The Europeans are used to countries which, however diversified they may be, are built more or less on the same pattern. They are historical conglomerations of various smaller people which gradually united under the centralizing domination of a more powerful or more influential conqueror. They are made up of provinces which have retained their original characteristics, but which have in most cases become static. In practically all of them the largest city is the political as well as the cultural capital.

There is, however, no such thing in America, and the more one lives and studies this continent, the greater one's sense of confusion.

An Englishman who has lived here many years said to me: 'My job keeps me in Washington, but Washington, of course, does not represent America. When I am in New York, I know also that New York is not America. In San Francisco, my American friends warn me that the Coast is not America. New England is not America; neither is the South. For a while I comforted myself in the belief that America was best represented by the Middle West. But now that I know the Middle West fairly well I have no particular reason to believe that it is more typical of what is really American than any other part of the country. After living ten years in America I still ask myself: Where is America? And my answer is that I don't know, and that I shall probably never find out.'

To look at a map of the United States is not helpful; the rectangular boundaries of the states are very disturbing to a European mind. We know that sectional patriotism is strong in the forty-eight states, even stronger in many ways than the regional idiosyncrasies of France, Germany, or England. But how can the inhabitants of these arbitrary rectangles actually feel a coincidence between one of the most primitive instincts of man—his attachment to his native land—and these geometric boundaries? Again one feels the same sense of abstraction which is so characteristic of America as a whole.

The truth is that the growth of the American sense of nationality has followed a course inverse to that of older countries. The European first becomes conscious of himself because he lives in a definite place where his forefathers lived before him, because he speaks a language which has always been spoken there, and because he feels a general sense of physical fixity in his surroundings. The *political* consequences of being a Frenchman, an Englishman, or an Italian are, in a sense, secondary manifestations of his nationality. They are superimposed.

But the Americans began to be *politically* conscious of being a nation before they felt that the land under their feet was really their homeland. It was only after they had broken off their allegiance to the British that they started—very slowly—to realize that America was the particular section of the planet to which they belonged, where their children and grandchildren would be born and would die. They began to grow roots after they were already in full bloom as an organized nation.

This—among others—is one of the important reasons why the Declaration of Independence is a certificate of birth not only for the whole American nation but for each American, even to-day; and why also the Constitution has always had a sacred character, for which there is no counterpart in any other country. It may be a wise political document, but it is even more important as the most genuine and most truly mystical source from which every American derives the consciousness of being himself. If the improbable choice were given to Americans by some great jokester, 'Would you prefer to go on living in your country and be deprived of your Constitution and everything that it stands for, or would you prefer to take it with you to some new wilderness?' I am not quite sure what the results of the referendum would be.

Most of the native Americans with three or four generations behind them forget that those who have come after them undergo a process of adaptation. It does not matter whether those who have crossed the seas are conscious of what takes place within themselves when they decide to be naturalized. It does not matter, either, whether they become Americans merely because they are tempted by better opportunities or because they were thrown out of their native land by persecution of one kind or another. The important fact is this: all those who are coming to-day and those who will come to-morrow are required first of all to accept a certain outlook on life and certain moral and political principles which will make them Americans. These things must take place in their minds and in their souls. Whether they adapt themselves to the landscape, to the architecture of the towns, to the food and drinks of their new country, is secondary. Whether they can speak its language is also not very important. The main thing is that they should be won over to Americanism, which is a set of moral and political doctrines.

Curiously enough, in a country where material changes are extraordinarily rapid, this moral and political frame has the stability of a dogma. For instance, America is the only country in the world which pretends to listen to the teaching of its founders as if they were still alive. Political battles of to-day are fought with arguments based on the speeches or writings of men dead over a century ago. Most Americans behave, in fact, as if men like Washington, Hamilton, Jefferson, and many others could be called up on the phone for advice. Their wisdom is considered as eternal as that of the Biblical prophets. To show how distinctively American this conception is, one has only to imagine what would happen if Mr. Chamberlain justified his present policy by quoting William Pitt, or if M. Daladier evoked the authority of Danton as a guide.

In fact, to become an American is a process which resembles a conversion. It is not so much a new country that one adopts as a new creed. And in all Americans can be discerned some of the traits of those who have, at one time or another, abandoned an ancient faith for a new one.

This explains, perhaps, the importance of the factor mentioned at the beginning of this article: that, in the make-up of an American, his defiance of the rest of the world, and particularly Europe, is fundamental and unavoidable. . . .

If the interpretation I have tried to give of what makes an American is not wholly wrong, it explains why the American is in a peculiar position in relation to the rest of the world. His conception of nationality makes him, in a way, better equipped to resist the degrading forces which are now at work in the world than the citizen of any other country. . . .

In the Progressive Party's platform published last April, for instance, one finds the following statement:—

'We believe that this hemisphere—all of it—was set aside by our Creator for the ultimate destiny of man. Here a vast continent was kept virgin for centuries. Here it was ordained that man should work out the final act in the greatest drama of life. From the Arctic to Cape Horn, let no foreign power trespass. Our hemisphere was divinely destined to evolve peace, security, and plenty. It shall remain inviolate for that sacred purpose.

This is a lofty conception, and the immigrant, the pioneer, the refugee, or the oppressed, whether he arrived here a century ago or last week, cannot help being heartened by such words. The question is, however, how much longer can the American maintain the posture of a man who stands on tiptoe on the ground because he feels it is his destiny to keep his head above the clouds?

II. ". . . .THAT ALL MEN ARE CREATED EQUAL. . . .

Have the self-evident truths put forth in the Declaration of Independence been realized in the United States? Has the proud assertion that all men are created equal left its stamp on the nation? Has it merely remained a dream or has it always been a hypocritical mask for ruthless exploiters of the weak and the powerless? These are some of the questions most foreign observers of the United States have felt a need to consider.

Few other nations have formulated so lofty goals for themselves. Of few other nations has so much been expected. This may be one set of reasons for the disappointment expressed by some observers and for the harsh criticism by others. But it would be misleading to explain all criticism of lack of equality in the United States with reference to ideals and images alone.

The shadow of black slavery still lies across American society. Racism is not a peculiarly American characteristic: on this score guilt seems evenly spread among the peoples of the earth. However, with its extremely heterogeneous population and the continuing throes of forging the many cultures, religions and races into a common nation, racism may be more visible in the United States than in many other countries. As Denis W. Brogan has put it in *The American Character*: "Not all Americans are at home in America or are accepted as first-class citizens. For America has not, any more than other countries have, found a means of uniting all its people on the basis of freedom. Its political and social tradition, which has so successfully set out to make men and women proud and glad to be Americans in this world, has not dealt or attempted to deal with all of human hopes and fears."

27

Further, there are the contradictions between ideals and social reality found in all capitalist societies with a liberal ideology.

In what sense were American children *"private things"* in 1906? Have they become more "public" since then? What slowed the process of child welfare legislation? Why is America's theory of freedom inadequate? Why do Americans desire titles and foreign honors? How would Americans respond to an "Emperor of the United States?" In what ways is America a "levelling" society? Has life in America, even after slavery, made black people forget about Africa? Why was John Clark so critical of American blacks? In what ways has American history been the story of class conflict?

HERBERT GEORGE WELLS
AN INADEQUATE THEORY OF FREEDOM

From the publication of his first volume of fiction in 1895, H. G. Wells (1866-1946) was deeply interested in The Shape of Things to Come *(1933). This interest led him, as it continues to lead so many others, to the United States which he visited for the first time in 1906. He went there, he wrote in his introductory chapter to* The Future in America: A Search after Realities *(London, 1906) "to find whatever consciousness or vague consciousness of a common purpose there may be, what is their Vision, their American Utopia, how much Will there is shaping to attain it, how much capacity goes with the will—what, in short, there is in America, over and above the mere mechanical consequences of scattering multitudes of energetic Europeans athwart a vast, healthy, productive and practically empty continent in the temperate zone." Although he found much to deplore and at times was "disposed to make that tall lady in New York Harbour stand as a symbol for the liberty of property," he finally concluded that "the balance of my mind tilts steadily to a belief in a continuing and accelerated progress now in human affairs."*

Again and again, Wells returned to the inadequacy of a liberal theory of freedom that fails to embrace large segments of the population who, because of class, race or ideology, are placed beyond the pale. The following chapter entitled "Certain Workers" is taken from

The Future in America, *pp. 147-157. Reprinted by permission of Arno Press, Inc., 1974.*

Now, in the preceding chapter I tried to convey my impression of the spending and wealth-getting of this vast community; I tried to convey how irresponsible it was, how unpremeditated. The American rich have, as it were, floated up out of a confused struggle of equal individuals. That individualistic commercial struggle has not only flung up these rich to their own and the world's amazement; it is also, with an equal blindness, crushing and maiming great multitudes of souls. But this is a fact that does not smite upon one's attention at the outset. The English visitor to the great towns sees the spending, sees the general prosperity, the universal air of confident pride; he must go out of his way to find the underside to these things.

One little thing set me questioning. I had been one Sunday night down town, supping and talking with Mr. Abraham Cahan about "East Side," that strange city within a city, which has a drama of its own and a literature and a press, and about Russia and her problem, and I was returning on the subway about two o'clock in the morning. I became aware of a little lad sitting opposite me, a childish-faced, delicate little creature of eleven years old or thereabouts, wearing the uniform of a boy messenger. He drooped with fatigue, roused himself with a start, edged from his seat with a sigh, stepped off the car, and was vanishing upstairs into the electric glare of Astor Place as the train ran out of the station.

"What on earth," said I, "is that baby doing abroad at this time of night?"

For me this weary little wretch became the irritant centre of a painful region of inquiry. "How many hours a day may a child work in New York?" I began to ask people, "and when may a boy leave school?"

I had blundered, I found, upon the weakest spot in America's fine front of national well-being. My eyes were opened to the childish newsboys who sold me papers, and the little bootblacks at the street corners. Nocturnal child employment is a social abomination. I gathered stories of juvenile vice, of lads of nine and ten suffering from terrible diseases, of the contingent sent out of the ranks of these messengers to the hospitals and jails. I began to realize another aspect of that great theory of the liberty of property and the subordination of the state to business, upon which American institutions are based. That theory has no regard for children. Indeed, it is a theory that disregards women and children, the cardinal facts of life, altogether. They are in America *private things* . . .

It is curious how little we, who live in the dawning light of a new time, question the intellectual assumptions of the social order about us. We find ourselves in a life of huge confusions and many cruelties, we plan this and that to remedy and improve, but very few of us go down to the ideas that begot these ugly conditions, the laws, the usages and liberties that are now in their detailed expansion so perplexing, intricate, and overwhelming. Yet the life of man is altogether made up of will cast into the mould of ideas, and only by correcting ideas, changing ideas and replacing ideas, are any ameliorations and advances to be achieved in human destiny. All other things are subordinate to that.

Now, the theory of liberty upon which the liberalism of Great Britain, the Constitution of the United States, and the bourgeois republic of France rests, assumes that all men are free and equal. They are all tacitly supposed to be adult and immortal, they are sovereign over their property and over their wives and children, and everything is framed with a view to ensuring them security in the enjoyment of their rights. No doubt this was a better theory than that of the divine right of kings, against which it did triumphant battle; but it does, as one sees it to-day, fall most extraordinarily short of the truth, and only a few logical fanatics have ever tried to carry it out to its complete consequences. For example, it ignored the facts that more than half of the adult people in a country are women, and that all the men and women of a country taken together are hardly as numerous, and far less important to the welfare of that country, than the individuals under age. It regarded living as just living, a stupid dead-level of egotistical effort and enjoyment; it was blind to the fact that living is part growing, part learning, part dying to make way, and altogether service and sacrifice. It asserted that the care and education of children, and business bargains affecting the employment and welfare of women and children, are private affairs. It resisted the compulsory education of children, and factory legislation, therefore, with extraordinary persistence and bitterness. The common sense of the three great progressive nations concerned has been stronger than their theory, but to this day enormous social evils are to be traced to that passionate jealousy of state intervention between a man and his wife, his children, and other property, which is the distinctive unprecedented feature of the originally middle-class modern organization of society upon commercial and industrial conceptions in which we are all (and America most deeply) living.

I began with a drowsy little messenger boy in the New York subway. Before I had done with the question I had come upon amazing things. Just think of it! This richest, greatest country the world has ever seen has over 1,700,000 children under fifteen years of age toiling in fields, factories, mines, and workshops. And Robert Hunter, whose "Poverty," if I were autocrat, should be compulsory reading for every prosperous adult in the United States, tells me of "not less than eighty thousand children, most of whom are little girls, at present employed in the textile mills of this country. In the South there are now six times as many children at work as there were twenty years ago. Child labour is increasing yearly in that section of the country. Each year more little ones are brought in from the fields and hills to live in the degrading and demoralizing atmosphere of the mill towns . . ."

In the worst days of cotton-milling in England the conditions were hardly worse than those now existing in the South. Children, the tiniest and frailest, of five and six years of age, rise in the morning and, like old men and women, go to the mills to do their day's labour; and, when they return home, "wearily fling themselves on their beds, too tired to take off their clothes." Many children work all night—"in the maddening racket of the machinery, in an atmosphere insanitary and clouded with humidity and lint."

"It will be long," adds Mr. Hunter, in his description, "before I forget the face of a little boy of six years, with his hands stretched forward to rearrange a bit of machinery, his pallid face and spare form already showing the physical effects of labour. This child, six years of age, was working twelve hours a day.". . . .

Well, we English have no right to condemn the Americans for these things. The history of our own industrial development is black with the blood of tortured and murdered children. New Jersey sends her pauper children south to-day into worse than slavery, but, as Cottle tells in his reminiscences of Southey and Coleridge, that is precisely the same wretched export that Bristol packed off to feed the mills of Manchester in late Georgian times. We got ahead with factory legislation by no peculiar virtue in our statecraft, it was just the revenge the landlords took upon the manufacturers for reform and free trade in corn and food. In America the manufacturers have had things to themselves.

And America has difficulties to encounter of which we know nothing. In the matter of labour legislation, each state legislature is supreme; in each separate state the forces of light and progress must fight the battle of the children and the future over again against interests, lies, prejudice, and stupidity. Each state pleads the bad example of another state, and there is always the threat that capital will withdraw. No national minimum is possible under existing conditions. And when the laws have passed, there is still the universal contempt for state control to reckon with, the impossibilities of enforcement. Illinois, for instance, scandalized at the spectacle of children in those filthy stockyards, ankle-deep in blood, cleaning intestines and trimming meat, recently passed a Child Labour Law that raised the minimum age for such employment to sixteen, but evasion, they told me in Chicago, was simple and easy. New York, too, can show by its statute books that my drowsy, nocturnal messenger boy was illegal and impossible. . . .

This is the bottommost end of the scale that at the top has all the lavish spending of Fifth Avenue, the joyous, wanton giving of Mr. Andrew Carnegie. Equally with these things, it is an unpremeditated consequence of an inadequate theory of freedom. The foolish extravagances of the rich, the architectural bathos of Newport, the dingy, noisy, economic jumble of central and south Chicago, the Standard Oil offices in Broadway, the darkened streets beneath New York's elevated railroad, the littered ugliness of Niagara's banks, are all so many accordant aspects and inexorable consequences of the same undisciplined way of living. Let each man push for himself—it comes to these things. . . .

So far as our purpose of casting a horoscope goes, we have particularly to note this as affecting the future; these working children cannot be learning to read—though they will presently be having votes; they cannot grow up fit to bear arms, to be in any sense but a vile, corrupting sweater's sense—men. So miserably they will avenge themselves by supplying the stuff for vice, for crime, for yet more criminal political manipulations. One million seven hundred children, practically uneducated, are toiling over here, and growing up, darkened, marred, and dangerous, into the American Future I am seeking to forecast.

WU TINGFANG
AN AMERICAN EMPEROR?

The Chinese diplomat, Dr. Wu Tingfang, who stayed nearly eight years in the United States and also served his emperor in Europe, may at times strike present-day readers as somewhat naïve in his comments on America and the Americans From a Chinese Point of View *(London, 1914). Reprinted by permission of Gerald Duckworth & Co. Ltd. He was, for instance, concerned "that the independent and thoughtless way in which the American young people take on themselves the marriage vow does not as a rule result in suitable companionships," and thought "it would be a good policy if all young Americans, before definitely committing themselves to a promise of marriage, would at least consult their mothers, and ask them to make private and confidential inquiries as to the disposition, as well as to the moral and physical fitness of the young man or lady whom they contemplate marrying. Mothers are naturally concerned about the welfare and happiness of their offspring, and could be trusted in most cases to make careful, impartial and conscientious inquiries as to whether the girl or man was really a worthy and suitable life partner for their children." He tells of his unsuccessful attempt to convince a newly engaged couple, but "had to conclude that love is blind." He was also preoccupied with differences between the costumes of the two cultures and devoted several chapters and illustrations to an argument for the superiority of Chinese fashions.*

The following pages (84-87, 89-93) from his chapter on "American Freedom and Equality" underline his aristocratic as well as his formalistic way of thought.

* * *

The dislike of distinction of classes which arises from the principle of equality is apparent wherever you go in the States. The railroad cars are not marked first, second, or third, as they are in Europe. It is true that there are Pullman cars, and palace cars, with superior and superb accommodation, and for which the occupant has to pay an extra fare; but the outside of the car simply bears the name "Pullman" without indicating its class, and anyone who is willing to pay the fare may share its luxuries. I should mention that in some of the Southern states negroes are compelled to ride on separate cars. On one occasion, arriving at the railroad station in one of those states, I noticed there were two waiting-rooms, one labelled "For the White," and the other "For the Colored." The railway porter took my portmanteau to the room for the white, but my conscience soon whispered I had come to the wrong place, as neither of the two rooms was intended for people of my complexion. The street-cars are more democratic; there is no division of classes; all people, high or low, sit in the same car without distinction of race, color or sex. It is a common thing to see a workman, dressed in shabby clothes full of dirt, sitting next to a millionaire or a fashionable lady gorgeously clothed. Cabinet officers and their wives do not think it beneath their dignity to sit beside a laborer, or a coolie, as he is called in China.

Foreign Ministers and Ambassadors coming to Washington soon learn to follow these local customs. In a European country they ride in coronated carriages, with two livery-men; but in Washington they usually go about on foot, or travel by the streetcars. I frequently saw the late Lord Pauncefote, the celebrated British Ambassador to Washington, ride to the State Department in the street-car. My adoption of this democratic way of travelling during the time I was in America was the cause of a complaint being made against me at Peking. The complainants were certain Chinese high officials who had had occasion to visit the States; one of them had had a foreign education, and ought to have known better than to have joined in the accusation that my unpretentious manner of living was not becoming the dignity of a representative of China. They forgot that when in Rome you must do as the Romans do, and that to ride in a sumptuous carriage, with uniformed footmen, is in America not only an unnecessary expense, but a habit which, among such a democratic people as the Americans, would detract from, rather than add to, one's dignity.

. . . Of course, in a European Capital, where every diplomat drives in a carriage, I should follow the example of my colleagues. But even in England, I frequently met high statesmen, such, for example, as Lord Salisbury, walking in the streets. This unrestrained liberty and equality is remarkably conspicuous in the United States; for instance, at the White House official receptions or balls in Washington, I have seen ladies in ordinary dress, while on one occasion a woman appeared in the dress of a man. This was Doctor Mary Walker. . . .

There are no peers in the United States, as the Government has no power to create them; and although America is nominally a free country, yet if a foreign government should confer a decoration on an American citizen for services rendered, he cannot accept it without the consent of Congress, just as under a monarchy a subject must obtain his sovereign's permission to wear a foreign decoration. It is true that there are some such titled persons in America, but they are not treated with any greater respect or distinction than other citizens; yet you frequently find people in America who not only would not disdain, but are actually anxious, to receive decorations from foreign governments. Once, at least, an American high official, just before leaving the country to which he had been accredited, accepted, without permission, a decoration, knowing, that if he had asked for the consent of Congress, he would not have been allowed to receive it.

It is human nature to love change and variety, and for every person to be designated "Mister" is too tame and flat for the go-ahead Americans. Hence many of the people whom you meet daily have some prefix to their names, such as General, Colonel, Major, President, Judge, etc. You will not be far wrong to call a man "Judge" when he is a lawyer; or "General" or "Colonel" if he has served in the army; or "Admiral" or "Captain" if he has been in the navy. Though neither the Federal nor the State Government has power to confer titles, the magnates do so. They see that dukes and other peers are created in Europe, and that the partners in the big, wealthy firms over there, are called "merchant princes," and so to outdo them, they arrogate to themselves a still higher title. Hence there are railroad kings, copper kings, tobacco kings, etc. It is, however, manifestly improper and incongruous that the people should possess a higher title than their President, who is the head of the nation. To make it even, I would suggest that the title "President" be changed to "Emperor," for the following reasons: First, it would not only do away with the impropriety of the chief magistrate of the nation assuming a name below that of some of his people, but it would place him on a level with the highest ruler of any nation on the face of the earth. I have often heard the remark that the President of the United States is no more than a common citizen, elected for four years, and that on the expiration of his term he reverts to his former humble status of a private citizen; that he has nothing in common with the dignified majesty of an Emperor; but were the highest official of the United States to be in future officially known as Emperor, all these depreciatory remarks would fall to the ground. There is no reason whatever why he should not be so styled, as, by virtue of his high office, he possesses almost as much power as the most aristocratic ruler of any nation. Secondly, it would clearly demonstrate the sovereign power of the people; a people who could make and unmake an Emperor, would certainly be highly respected. Thirdly, the United States sends ambassadors to Germany, Austria, Russia, etc. According to international law, ambassadors have what is called the representative character, that is, they represent their sovereign by whom they are delegated, and are entitled to the same honors to which their constituent would be entitled were he personally present. In a Republic where the head of the State is only a citizen and the sovereign is the people, it is only by a stretch of imagination that its ambassador can be said to represent the person of his soverign. Now it would be much more in consonance with the dignified character of an American ambassador to be the representative of an Emperor than of a simple President. The name of Emperor may be distasteful to some, but may not a new meaning be given to it? A word usually has several definitions. Now, if Congress were to pass a law authorizing the chief magistrate of the United States of America to be styled Emperor, such designation to mean nothing more than the word "President," the title would soon be understood in that sense. There is no reason in history or philology why the word "Emperor" should never mean anything other than a hereditary ruler. I make this suggestion seriously, and hope it will be adopted.

OMER CELAL SARC
A DEMOCRATIC SPIRIT

In 1957 Omer Celâl Sarc, a distinguished Turkish economist and one time rektor *of the University of Istanbul, and nineteen other recent visitors to the United States from different areas of the world were invited to contribute to a collection of essays:* As Others See Us: The United States Through Foreign Eyes *(1959). They were all asked to consider the following questions: "First, in what respects has your stay in the United States changed your former ideas about the United States and its People? Second, how does your present view of the United States and its people compare with that held in your country. . . ? Third, what, in your opinion, can the people of your country and the United States learn from each other?"*

The following extract from Dr. Sarc's essay, (pp. 132-134, 140-142) is evidence not only of his largely positive reactions to the state of affairs in this country but of his optimistic view of its future possibilities. Throughout his essay his approach is comparative, and he may thus serve as a reminder that the United States, by natives and foreigners alike, is frequently judged by an absolute and idealized standard.

Selections from Omer Celâl Sarc, "From Turkey," in Franz M. Joseph, As Others See Us: The United States Through Foreign Eyes *(copyright © 1959 by Princeton University Press), pp. 132-134, 140-142. Reprinted by permission of Princeton University Press.*

One of the distinctive traits of the American people which the foreign visitor remarks is the prevailing democratic-folksy spirit. In contrast to some other countries, class consciousness among higher ranking persons is weak if not absent. People are not ashamed of a humble origin, but rather tend to be proud of it if they have made headway in life. The tone adopted toward the small man is neither paternal and condescending nor cool and reserved, and his own attitude is characterized by a total absence of servility and of any inhibitions or aggressiveness arising from a sense of inferiority. Persons in the higher layers of society usually like to chat about weather and sports events with lower-ranking people, such as shopkeepers and waiters, and handshakes are often exchanged.

Not only is the small man not disdained, but some of his standards seem to gain ground at the expense of those of the elite. Thus in many fields demeanor appears to have become increasingly less formal. Persons are often addressed as "Mac," audiences as "folks." Even bosses and subordinates are soon on a first-name basis. On her latest visit to the United States the Queen of England was greeted, I hear, with cheers of "Hi, Liz." Dressing also becomes more and more informal. The top hat and the white tie are almost obsolete. In summer a growing number of men renounce neckties and wear short-sleeved shirts, an attire for which American tourists in more sophisticated Europe have sometimes been criticized. The trend manifests itself in language too. In many countries the speech of the elite is the model that the majority strives to follow, since it is regarded as a mark of high social standing. In America, on the other hand, the speech of the masses appears to have a greater appeal. I had the impression that the elite, instead of attempting to defend its way of speaking, tends to flirt with the popular idiom, by readily adopting neologisms and often using slang. There are of course groups where formality still prevails, rank counts, and attention is paid to descent, for example to the length of time since the family's first acquisition of wealth or since its arrival in the United States. But the numerical importance of these groups is slight and decreasing. It appears that by reason of the country's history and political structure this democratic spirit has always been inherent in America, but that in the decades past it has become stronger. This may be because the growing purchasing power of the masses, combined with their enormous voting power, not only makes it mandatory to take their preferences into account in business and politics but contributes to a diffusion of their standards in other domains as well.

Of course this democratic spirit does not imply a general recognition of the equality of all human beings. Racial prejudices still exist in parts of the population. In the South some people tend to regard the Negro as inferior, while others, though recognizing his equality, do not wish to associate with him in everyday life. Even in the North, apparently, there is sometimes a reluctance to have Negroes as neighbors, and I understand that real-estate prices ultimately fall in quarters into which Negroes move. I think, however, that the extent of racial prejudice in America and the difficulties in the Negro's situation are usually exaggerated abroad. The regrettable incidents that sometimes occur are easily generalized, while certain other facts are overlooked. In the first place, there is no country that is entirely free of some such prejudices. Second, the problem is particularly complicated in the United States by its relatively high percentage of Negroes in the total population. Furthermore, anti-Negro feeling is declining. Great efforts are being made toward overcoming racial prejudices, efforts that can be said to reflect the American people's strong sense of right and wrong. Considerable progress has been made in assuring Negroes equal treatment in most fields, partly by resorting to legislative measures. The material situation of the Negro population, though not so good as that of the white, especially with regard to dwellings, is by no means bad compared with other countries. Its income has increased with rising general prosperity. In the parts of America I visited—the northern and western states—Negroes in no way left on me the impression of a persecuted race. . . .

It was a great surprise for me not to find in America marked class differences, allegedly a fundamental attribute of a capitalistic society. Some poverty certainly exists. I know of the "Tobacco Road" conditions in the deep South and the hillbilly regions in the Appalachians, and have seen destitute quarters in cities. Before the Second World War about forty percent of the population appears to have had only enough income to make possible bare subsistence—measured of course by American standards. But since then the amazing increase in national income has mostly benefited the poor, and there has been a sharp decrease in the percentage of families unable to provide more than mere subsistence. At the same time the very rich have become somewhat poorer, mainly because of sharply progressive income and inheritance tax rates and to some extent through a decline in the interest rate. As a result, a large-scale equalization has taken place, which manifests itself in the tremendous absolute and relative expansion of the middle class. At present the income of perhaps two-thirds of American families appears to be above the level necessary to assure adequate diet and clothing, some medical and dental care, and a certain amount of entertainment and comfort. Many enjoy in addition the benefits of social security.

Of these families only a very small proportion are really rich, say with a yearly net income of $15,000 or more, and among the remainder, constituting the bulk of the population, differences in living standards are slight. The families in this large group can afford neither servants nor custom-made suits, but practically all own a motorcar and a refrigerator, and have lodgings that are adequate in at least certain respects, for instance well heated in winter. In this immense middle class the main difference in living standards seems to be that certain durables (television, air-conditioning sets, movie cameras) and certain possibilities (trips to Europe, college education for children) are available to some but not to all.

This relatively equal distribution of income constitutes at present one of the distinguishing features of American society. Turkey does not belong among the countries with the greatest inequality in income distribution; the masses there are poor, but their poverty is not so great as elsewhere (they are at least not undernourished and do not lack footwear), nor is the wealth of the rich comparable with that in some other countries. Nevertheless the range of differences is much larger than in the United States. In America the difference between a university professor's standard of living and that of a factory worker is one of degree, but in Turkey it is fundamental, affecting housing, furniture, clothing, and medical care, not to speak of the education given to children. In fact the worker in Turkey does not belong to the middle class. Since marked disparities in living standards are an important barrier to genuine fraternization between individuals, it can be said that the equalization of income distribution has greatly consolidated democracy in America.

Moreover, this has been achieved mainly by an upward leveling. Though the average income of the very rich has somewhat declined, the increment in that of the masses has come very little, if at all, from taxes collected from the rich. Its principle source has been the large increase in national income; both legislation and trade-union action have provided labor with a growing proportion of this increase.

J. P. CLARK
THE BLACKS

John Pepper Clark, Nigerian poet and playwright, was invited to come to Princeton University as a fellow of a privately financed pro-

gram with the aim of introducing American civilization to the intel-
ligensia of other countries. He did not like much of what he saw and,
to put it mildly, did not get along well with his hosts. Before the
year's program was terminated he was asked to leave.

The book he wrote about his experience, America, Their America
(London, 1964), is, to quote from the forward by Professor E. U.
Essien-Udom, "an important commentary on contemporary American
society, and especially on the massive efforts of the United States
policy-makers to make friends and influence people abroad."

The fact that he was black did not make J. P. Clark less critical
when evaluating the cultural and social life of Americans of African
descent. While he gave vent to his undisguised disgust with the racist
attitudes of white Americans, he also found that "there was so much
that was wrong with the house of the blacks in America, even among
themselves and on the level of artists, that the most well-mannered
cousin calling from abroad could not help but be openly critical—un-
less of course a primitive pride in the family and an equally primitive
urge to clean it out and make the place better for all were lacking."

The following views on black culture in North America form the
conclusion of his chapter on "The Blacks," pp. 74-84 of the 1968
edition published by Heinemann in The African Writers Series.
Copyright © 1964 by André Deutsch Ltd. Permission to reprint
granted by copyright holder.

Typical and at once unique is the American Society for African
Culture all very well set up in down-town New York. As is evident
from its name, the society does not present a broad front in the fight
to attain for the Negro an equal place, taken for granted in his native
American society. Rather, the big point those in it make is the home
they have found anew in Africa. Thus its sponsors, most of them Lincoln [University] alumni, would shut out even those whites with
genuine interest and perhaps better knowledge of Africa, a restriction
and reverse bias that should stand the society in good stead if ever
it comes out for sit-ins, freedom-rides, street demonstrations, and
popular expressions of that kind, as the very respectable and gouty
NAACP has had to do recently. But fortunately for AMSAC, it is
always in better company and far removed from the bad breath and
sweat of the man uptown in Harlem. Like some bored old lady with
a lot of money and who is always scared to be alone by herself, the

society is for ever thinking up some party or platform. And it has a nose that smells out an honoured guest from abroad even before he has set foot on US soil. Every leader of any delegation from Africa, preferably in sumptuous agbada or kente, is sedulously scouted out, courted and asked over by AMSAC to a party for which he pays with an address, often with only very little to do with culture except in the widest sense of the word. And of course no artist from Africa, on a grant the society knows little of or cares little about emulating, is ever missed on the list of notables the society constantly compiles to its credit, comfort and complacency.

In such circumstances, it matters very little if the religious and social significance of an original Bambara head-piece copied and proudly hung up on the wall of the AMSAC centre is completely lost and forgotten there. Perhaps it had not even been recognized to begin with. Indeed the mix-up and masquerade could be most crushing. The story goes that on one occasion the proud AMSAC host actually slapped on the back the honourable gentleman from Gabon and asked in great cheer how the old capital city of all the Congos was doing after that maverick [Patrice] Lumumba!

Most symptomatic of the social-climbing and status-seeking habits that probably provide the strongest driving force behind the AMSAC was that grand ball it gave last Christmas for all African ambassadors to the United Nations. Like the great festival of folly with which the society had earlier sought fame in Lagos, the gala affair featured luminaries and debutantes but gave little or no room to undiscovered stars and ordinary folks teeming in the ghettos of Harlem, perhaps for fear they might darken the gleaming hall and gates of the Hotel Americana. All was white ties and tails and mink stoles, and the fabulous Duke Ellington himself was there with his band to serenade everybody into dreamland. But not much dancing was done that night since everybody who was anybody or as likely as not part of that bleak stratum of society starved of high cocktail occasions, made sure of a place on the floor so as not to lose for another season or life this one chance of rubbing shoulders with the great of the land. With me that night was my friend James Ward, an old boy of Princeton only now beginning to put his weight behind the lever to upturn for once and all the oppressive burden his black people have had to bear all these many years. And between us sat in dazzling dress his old girl friend of schooldays in Philadelphia. They seemed quite overwhelmed with all the pomp and circumstance of the occasion, especially during the pompous roll-call of honoured guests present. First of them all, it turned out amid great cheers, was the distinguished US Ambassador to the UN, Mr Adlai Stevenson. The great man was even prevailed upon to make a speech and was walked to the rostrum by the super-host of the occasion Dr John A. Davis, all beaming and sweating with satisfaction. Later, when Duke struck up another tune well-remembered with tears by many, and when hosts and guests began shuffling on their feet and basking in all the limelight, Dr Davis and the partner in his arms stopped graciously in front of me.

'Meet my wife,' he said. We exchanged how-do-you-do, after which he kindly added: 'Have a dance with her.' I shook my head, and he asked why not. Without thought, I told him there and then I was disappointed in the whole show. Both husband and wife looked appropriately shocked, and appeared not to understand. So that in quick succession I asked: Why the build-up for the American Stevenson? How was it not one of his excellent friends from Africa had been given a similar opportunity of saying a word or two, or wasn't the party for them after all, but in fact for Ambassador Stevenson? And if he had to speak at all as the home representative, should that not be after the doyen among the African guests of honour had had the floor? Or was it simply giving the great man a big hand, which he needed somewhat, after being mauled and daubed a dove and an appeaser in the Cuba eyeball-to-eyeball aftermath? Undoubtedly I had goofed, but the Davis couple took it all very politely, and as they resumed dancing and fell back among the convivial crowd on the floor, the man suddenly brightened up and said laughingly over his wife's fair shoulders that I might probably be correct about the tail-end of my query.

From the upper middle-class club of AMSAC to the 'family' night gatherings that branches of the New York Public Library in Harlem sponsor in a sort of healthy rivalry among themselves, it is not really a long walk. These occasions, usually ones of friendly encounter, sometimes between local writers and their readers, and at other times on a triangular level with visiting African authors brought in, provide a 'culture' dose for those of the lower income brackets herded in Harlem as junkets downtown cater for the dilettanti whose one distinction, to quote Frazier, is an indisputable capacity for conspicuous consumption. Apart from that, the taste and indeed the fare are the same between both circles. Each asked me over as a speaking guest, and on each 'at home' host and guest were happy to part, never to cultivate each other's company again. Such was the unpleasantness and nausea felt on both sides, a professional hostess, who floats promotion parties for upcoming artists of all kinds, called for her smelling salts, took a sniff or two as my grandmother would her snuff, and turning to an equally embarrassed friend at one of these affairs, said in everybody's hearing: 'Of course, the young man may be a genius. But how can I possibly ask friends over to meet him when he shows such a penchant for making enemies?'

There was so much that was wrong with the house of the blacks in America, even among themselves and on the level of artists, that the most well-mannered cousin calling from abroad could not help but be openly critical—unless of course a primitive pride in the family and an equally primitive urge to clean it out and make the place better for all were lacking. It was a unique and rich experience sharing with the black citizens of America their growing excitement and sense of discovery towards Africa, a place only vaguely remembered by them before, and that with absolute shame and horror, from memories of an irrevocable fall, as Christians years ago recalled the doings in the Garden of Eden. Now, not only has this place they had been taught all their lives to look upon as a jungle full of fatal fruits and serpents turned out to be a rich and open plantation farmed all along by foreign squatters for their own benefit, but the black sons of the soil have at last actually risen and driven the exploiters back across the seas from where they came. And it was no mean or distant performances that could be kept out or distorted for the ears of the people. Today, even the bum on Harlem's 125th Street, although he may not be able to read the *New York Times* that prints all the news that is fit to print, and although he may not own a TV set to tune to community-minded stations, can see with his own eyes all the black diplomats at the UN.

Going from one independent country in Africa to another still burning to have its turn, I had observed a similar sense of vicarious satisfaction and feeling of elation that the enemy is at least out of the city gates, although other than those one is defending. In the United States, however, the joy appears even more intense among the emergent Negro. Their goal, though is not the African one of expelling the host, but that of kitchenmen, laundry-hands, motor-boys and non-coms, all of them long restricted to the lowest ranks in the armed forces for no just and legitimate cause, demanding at long last a fair share in the victory and spoils with colleagues really having no special abilities and merits to set them up and apart in permanent positions of privilege.

Out of this new emotional response to Africa among the Negro in America has come a great love for everything African. It is all very heart-warming that a Negro can now get up today and declare the roots of his origin even if he cannot be as definite or far-reaching as President Kennedy disclosing his Irish ancestry to Newark voters also of that extraction. But when he goes collecting masks, and imita-tions at that, without knowing their religious and social symbols and observance; when he goes sporting drums, called over there tom-toms, in blissful belief that anybody can beat on them, however different in kind and intention, and produce the famous talk for all to grin at; if he goes collecting music from Africa and proclaiming each piece 'simple' and 'folksy'; then such an 'Afro-American', making a profes-sion of his faith among the uninitiated, more silly than cynical, must be called to order before he misleads himself and others into total perdition.

A greater danger still is the habit of identifying this phoney, gushing business partly or wholly with the genuine historical stand of Neg-ritude as established by Aimé Césaire and Leopold Senghor, or with the African Personality, to use Kwame Nkrumah's flamboyant slogan, which is better known in the States. There is an interesting feed-back here. The idea of the African Personality, especially in its political context, derived of course from the Pan-African Movement of Marcus Garvey and Dr Du Bois, and although both prophets naturally were never ones to listen to each other, it was to the lost black people of America they preached their sermons of Africa that must be redeemed, of an exodus back there, and of the glory and splendour that were its past. It is an irony of fate that today the black educated of America should be falling back upon the very doctrine they rejected and pooh-poohed half a century or so back. That they helped to hurl stones at both wisemen and still would deride them today should the two appear in Alabama or New York City may seem overstating the point. But both men are hardly ever remembered except by a few doubtful faithfuls squabbling on the fringe of Harlem's murky streets and slums. And more still, the spirit of union which has consecrated for better for worse several heroes and leaders in Africa, providing for each of their people a pivotal point, has apparently either by-passed America or presented her with so many candidates that they confound themselves.

On the other hand, what seems to dominate the field on the cultural front is the tendency among writers, editors and critics, college professors within the cult not excluded, to form themselves into associations for mutual promotion and admiration. As a pure reaction against a society that either from sheer indifference or discrimination strains from its main stream of literature works by Negro authors, this, like Negritude, would be a welcome stand and declaration, to create fresh new pools and channels out to sea. Unfortunately the current does not seem to be clear or cutting deep. Rather members of the club, swimmers, trainers and spectators alike, apparently prefer playing their own brand of game which is not bad, except that poor performances and low standards are everywhere applauded to the sky for the simple reason that they are by fellow members of the camp. And to thicken the cheers are the voices of patrons and promoters who naturally must be listened to and respected. Since everybody knows the rules, the patrons and promoters, usually honorary members from outside, play back the game by every time repeating the same fatuous and harmless platitudes and stereotypes like: 'negro writers express deep feelings,' 'the characters they create carry great humour and human warmth,' and 'the Negro hero is a simple, sweet soul.' All of this may be true but not the speciality or preserve of the Negro writer and people. And this is typical of the rich larding these people apply on their skin, a possible attempt to heighten or hide its existence.

Club members seeking compensation for a complex that shows them poor flounderers in life's stream of conflicting identities and links sometimes ask new-found associates from Africa whether there are any excavations for ancient and lost civilizations going on there, and if so, whether bards have sung them in epics. Not satisfied with the totem in hand, they would have broken pillars and parchments to convince denigrators like Senator Ellender that their black folks and cousins back in Africa did own and create something! At a Langston

Hughes party in Harlem, I even heard the further claim that the first American cowboy, not just in literature but in real life and history, was a Negro. Like jazz and other great contributions of the Negro people to American culture, the whites had promptly seized upon it and stolen the patent. A most reassuring claim that was, especially as it came from Professor Rosey Poole, a white woman promoter of the association.

Under such pull and push, it is a miracle writers of real worth have emerged at all among the Negroes. The lately over-lionized James Baldwin, the long silent Ralph Ellison, and self-effacing Sam Allen who really is the poet Paul Vessey, and Papa Langston Hughes himself, everywhere styled the poet-laureate of the Negro people and the Shakespeare of Harlem, easily come to mind. But even these are often loved for the wrong works and for reasons merely sociological and extra-literary and artistic. Poetry, they say, should get as near as possible to music, but when music is made to replace poetry, then it is another matter entirely. Thus it is very painful to hear critics, otherwise perfectly sound and intelligent, picking on the 'blues' of Langston Hughes as examples of his best work when there is evidently a corpus of good poetry to the man. But such pieces are as much chosen for the 'authentic manner' in which they reproduce the 'idiom and rhythm' of the blues as for the virtue they make of being black, and black to the palms and bottom.

Undoubtedly, the temptation of the one theme and motif to choose and of what apparatus and form to present it in overwhelms many a writer, but more so should he happen to be black, and therefore of Africa or America. The tendency I found much more among black authors in America than in Africa, where it is menace enough, is to fall for the blackness of it and forget all art. In Africa both publishers and public unabashedly give a strong impression of praying for this to happen, but then it is a gimmick to be expected, as a great majority of them are at present European, and therefore still have to get out of that terrible hangover feeling of being in a special relationship with exotic and simple natives. Little wonder a lot of people today are making capital out of the theme of encounter, that is, of black meeting white, and the conflict and complication therefrom for the African. All this is fine timber. But it still requires a good carpenter and cabinet maker to turn it into beautiful furniture. Unless one is a gifted and genuine craftsman, what comes to pass for a work of art is a wobbly, ugly stool that should better have remained the piece of log it was before the author began hacking it around. And such logs do in fact make extraordinary seating in the square and market place in front of the ancestral hall.

Coming to the States, where indigenous publishing and a literate, local reading public should really be no problem, the black-white theme takes on fresh colorations, albeit of a leprous kind! The point, often so belaboured from the defending end here, is not that Negro authors write only about the Negro. Who else can any author write for and about except his own people he knows so well? The real quarrel is that most Negro writers see their subject at one point and position only—that of protest and prayer. As a result and perhaps without any intention of so doing, they have helped to create and establish a fresh set of stereotype figures and faces capable of expressing only certain simple emotions and gestures, none of which has to do with anything complex or cerebral, or with the mystery and permanence of the mask.

On the contrary, like the one-piece orchestra whose sole member is a piano, so much effort and energy has gone into pounding out of it the desired harmony, that spectators, especially if they pay to get admitted to the concert as is usually the practice, may well be forgiven and indeed praised for honesty and integrity if they hiss and grow restless on their seats at false notes and an undistinguished, in fact, appalling performance. A cry of 'Take to the cornet!' from somewhere in the audience would then be a brotherly act, not the taunting of a perverse critic. But that exactly was the angry reaction at a Harlem meeting to a suggestion of mine that for a picture of the Negro as a problem in his country it would be a far more rewarding exercise and experience to depend on a trained social scientist who documents the case with living facts rather than on some novelist palming off an ill-dressed and undigested story out of which sticks the contended bone of colour. An artist if anything should be an inventor, a creator of new things with use and beauty out of ordinary familiar pieces and material lying around. If he is content merely to rehash or dress up old stocks and frames better left alone or which anybody can perfectly well ham up if they have a mind to, then all distinction falls down, and we are again among the tinkerers and salesmen.

Rejection, however and not in the arts alone, is rotten eggs and tomatoes to a group protesting genuine identity, and demanding respect and recognition that ought to have been theirs by right of birth as human beings and citizens of the United States. Such natural acceptance and respect should not be a payment or bonus awarded to a few acquiring the right accent and desk. And when it has been so for as long as grandmother can remember, bottles and bricks should be expected in return—which is the healthy, virile, development now breaking out all over the American field and front.

But to borrow an image from James Baldwin, which he in turn was probably not echoing from the old spiritual but unconsciously from the Prophet Elijah's address to the first Black Moslem convention in Washington, the great fire to follow from bitterness, if not now directed and kept in control, will certainly carry disaster for all. For who is it to be turned upon? Upon the whites, of course, who bought the black-man and have kept him ever since in one form of chain or another in the land of the free. But what of the blackman's brother in Africa who sold him into slavery for a few tinsels and drink? And the Negro himself who all these years has been content to rattle his shackles, to breed behind the bars of discrimination, and to regard the debilitating cobwebs of so-called toleration drifting in Northern cities and states as the earnest of the covenant long promised in the skies. Joseph the Dreamer rose out of bondage to greatness and embraced his brothers who sold him into slavery, and they say, even forgave his foreign master Potiphar and the mistress who sought the damnation of his soul. Hearing Malcolm X, the Black Moslem torch bearer, the Reverend Martin Luther King, Junior, who had just been bombed out of his home, and Dr Roy Wilkins of the NAACP all address the first ever united front Negro meeting at Harlem's 125th Street, it was to me as clear as the rain that was pouring then that the leaders spoke in different tongues. Which of them was understood by the huge section of the audience that defied the path of thunder and lightning to hear the case for action, it is still too presumptuous to tell.

VITALY KORIONOV
THE PATH OF THE AMERICAN WORKERS

*To what degree does our image of our country's past, its political
and social traditions, depend on the answers implicit in the historians'
questions, on their methods as well as their ideologies? Certainly the
study of historiography, of the way in which successive generations
of historians have interpreted what is frequently the same body of historical "facts," should have a sobering effect on the student of history.*

*Is the dominant theme of American history that of class struggle?
Although class struggle is the underlying principle of history for all
Marxists, who may therefore be expected to exaggerate its importance,
we would do well to consider whether other historians, for other
reasons, have tended to dismiss this factor altogether. Certainly the
class struggle, as dramatized by the labor unrest and strikes at the
turn of the century, has been as violent in the United States as in
most European countries.*

*The following excerpt is taken from a review by Vitaly Korionov
which appeared in the Russian newspaper* Pravda *on December 1,
1971. It has been translated and condensed in* The Current Digest
of the Soviet Press, *XXIII, no. 48 (Dec. 28, 1971), p. 26. Translation
copyright 1974 by* The Current Digest of the Soviet Press, *published
weekly at the Ohio State University by the American Association for
the Advancement of Slavic Studies; reprinted by permission of the Digest.*

. . . In particular, "The History of the Workers' Movement in the
U.S.A. in Recent Times," a two-volume work by a collective of
Soviet scholars, is a valuable work on the question [of the develop-
ment of the American labor movement].

The above-mentioned work covers the years 1918-1965, a very
complex period in the development of the workers' movement in the
United States. . . .

The Program of the Communist Party U.S.A. says : "In the process
of its historical development, the American working class has been
marked by its militant spirit and fighting capacity, which have been
displayed in countless battles; it has accumulated both great organiza-

tional experience and skills. But a certain political and ideological backwardness has hindered its successes.'' The authors of the two-volume work convincingly depict this ambivalent path traversed by the American workers' movement.

The book describes the peculiarities of the socioeconomic and political conditions in which the U.S. workers' movement has been developing and shows that the American proletarian has resisted a powerful, experienced and organized bourgeoisie that is growing fat on the sweat and blood of working people in the United States and many other countries.

The two-volume work shows that the whole history of the U.S.A. is a history of class struggle. It describes the class battles of 1918-19, which were greatly influenced by the ideas of the Great October Revolution; it describes the mighty demonstrations of the working people of the U.S.A. in the period of economic crisis and depression of the '30s, which were characterized by an unprecedented sweeping movement of jobless workers, strikes and the establishment of industrial trade unions.

Data on the vast scope of the U.S. working class's strike movement refute the myth that the class struggle has been "abating" in the United States. In the U.S.A. from 1918 to 1965 there were 143,853 strikes, in which 74,998,000 workers participated. As a result, 972, 800,000 man-hours were lost.

One of the most serious difficulties the U.S. working-class movement has been confronting for decades is the policy of "class partnership" pursued by the top leadership of the American labor unions affiliated with the A.F.L.-C.I.O., a leadership personified by the G. Meany group, which has chained itself to the chariot of U.S. imperialism's anti-people policy. . . .

The work under review speaks of the repeated attempts of the advanced forces of the U.S. workers movement to lead the working people out of the two-party cage by setting up a third party capable of pursuing an independent, progressive policy.

The efforts to lead the American workers' movement onto the broad path of active political struggle has encountered fierce resistance from imperialist forces and their agents within the workers' movement. Anticommunist and antilabor legislation, a ban on the Communist Party, the mass dismissals of Communists and other progressive workers have become the standard methods of operations of the imperialist governments for maintaining their control. In the United States this manifested itself quite graphically in the years of McCarthyism, when the rampage of Black Hundred reactionaries became the ruling circles' "standard of behavior." Using such political gangsters as McCarthy, the U.S. ruling class strived to smash the workers' movement, to suppress the black people's liberation movement, and to sweep away the vestiges of democratic freedoms.

The main blow was spearheaded against the vanguard of the working-class—the Communist Party U.S.A.—and above all, against its leadership cadres. Anticommunist dracome laws, one harsher than the next, flowed from Capital Hill in Washington as if from a horn of plenty. In accordance with the Smith Act the F.B.I. from July, 1948, arrested more than 140 officials of the Cummunist Party, in addition up to 400 American Communists of foreign extraction were deported from the United States.

The book shows the Communist Party U.S.A.'s place and role in the American workers' movement and describes the courageous struggle of its leadership to build and solidify the party on the principles of Marxism-Leninism and proletarian internationalism and especially against an old enemy of the revolutionary workers' movement, right-wing deviation. . . .

In the United States the social and political crisis—exacerbated by the aggressive war in Vietnam, racial clashes and mounting crisis phenomena in the economy—has been deepening. Demonstrations by young people have gained scope, while the antimonopoly movement has been rising to a new level. The upsurge of the mass struggle in the U.S.A. reflects the depth of the crisis in American capitalism. These processes should have been elucidated more extensively in the book under review.

Individual shortcomings, however, do not belittle the scholarly value of this work. Undoubtedly "The History of the Workers' Movement in the U.S.A. in Recent Times" will be read with interest by all who are stirred by problems of the most revolutionary class of our era, the working class.

III. DIVERSITY OR REGIMENTATION

At first glance, diversity would seem to be a characteristic feature of American society, a gigantic congregation of peoples from all over the world who have brought with them their various languages, religions and cultural traditions. And yet many observers have been impressed by the standardization and regimentation of life in America. In the face of such different conclusions, one may wonder whether all the visitor sees is his own preconceived notion of what the United States is like.

There is, however, also the possibility that the most divergent opinions may be given their due, that America can appear in so many disguises because it actually and potentially is so many different things. One may, like the British author Anthony Bailey (*In the Village,* 1972), immerse oneself in small-town New England and come so close to the individuals who make up that many-faceted community that generalizations about American civilization become pointless if not impossible. But the experience of Anthony Bailey in Stonington, Connecticut need not contradict the perceptive analysis by his compatriot Francis Williams (*"The American Invasion,* 1962) of, for instance, the lessons of McCarthyism: "It was not just the fear of Communism that gave McCarthy his power, although this provided him with his opportunity and his theme. There was an even more corroding fear: the fear of standing against the stream, of being suspected of being unsound, of being tabbed with the wrong label. The fear of the junior executive of his boss, of his ambitious wife of what the leader of local society would think, of both of the disapproval of their crowd. The fear of being an individual and of being alone."

Disagreement about the question of diversity or regimentation, then, may not be only a reflection of the different points of view of the beholders but of conflicting tendencies in American society. What forces in American life have made for diversity? for regimentation? What losses have Americans suffered in achieving their high material standard of living? What dangers to human life potentially exist in a "materialistic society, organised to produce things rather than people?" In what ways has quantity replaced quality, both in products and people? In what ways has efficiency replaced individuality in institutions other than the factory? What would Gandhi have said of "Fordism?" of "Soul engineers?" How secure are a people who "can be led, but will not be driven?"

ANDRE SIEGFRIED
SUPER-COLLECTIVISM

"Fordism"—mass production for the mass consumer—has for many foreign observers been the essence of the American industrial and economic revolution. French writers in particular have been engrossed by the effects of mass production on American society and its portents for Europe. Georges Duhamel spoke for many of his colleagues in America the Menace *(1931) when he regretted "the progressive approximation of human life to what we know of the way of life of insects—the same effacement of the individual, the same progressive reduction and unification of social types, the same organization of the group into special castes. . . ." Copyright 1931 by Houghton Mifflin Company. Copyright © renewed 1959 by Houghton Mifflin Company. Reprinted by permission of Houghton Mifflin Company. Here, as elsewhere in his rambling diatribe, Duhamel sounds a hysterical note, but even his countryman R. L. Bruckberger, whose* The Image of America *(1959) is an extremely favorable study of American civilization and who praises Ford as one of the great innovators of our time, warns that Ford's system as well as some aspects of his ideas may have totalitarian implications.*

*The French political scientist André Siegfried (1875-1959) was one of the most thorough and well-informed of America's many observers from abroad; beside the British diplomat James Bryce (*The American

Commonwealth, *1888) he comes closest to attaining the reputation of the still unsurpassed Alexis de Tocqueville. The following pages are taken from his concluding chapter, "European vs. American Civilization,"* in America Comes of Age: A French Analysis, *Translated by H. H. and Doris Hemming (London: Jonathan Cape Ltd, 1930; 1st ed. 1927) pp. 341-347.*

The America that Columbus discovered was to our ancestors geographically a new world. To-day, as a result of the revolutionary changes brought about by modern methods of production, it has again become a new world, and furthermore we have still to rediscover it.

Having first cleared away all hampering traditions and political obstacles, the American people are now creating on a vast scale an entirely original social structure which bears only a superficial resemblance to the European. It may even be a new age, an age in which Europe is to be relegated to a niche in the history of mankind; for Europe is no longer the driving force of the world. The old European civilisation did not really cross the Atlantic, for the American reawakening is not, as is generally supposed, simply a matter of degrees and dimensions; it is the creation of new conceptions. Many of the most magnificent material achievements of the United States have been made possible only by sacrificing certain rights of the individual, rights which we in the Old World regard as among the most precious victories of civilisation. In spite of their identical religious and ethnic origin, Europe and America are diverging in their respective scales of value. This contrast was brought to a head by the War, which installed the United States prematurely in an unassailable position of economic supremacy. To America the advent of the new order is a cause for pride, but to Europe it brings heart-burnings and regrets for a state of society that is doomed to disappear.

From an economic point of view, America is sane and healthy. Her prosperity in spite of possible set-backs rests on her vast natural resources and on the unexcelled efficiency of her means of production. Thanks to the abundance of her raw materials, her conquest of wealth has reached a point unknown elsewhere. To the American, Europe is a land of paupers, and Asia a continent of starving wretches. Luxury in everyday consumption and the extension to the many living conditions previously reserved for the few—these are new phenomena in the history of mankind, and are undoubtedly evidence of splendid progress. But what is absolutely new about this society which is accomplishing such marvels is that in all its many aspects—even including idealism and religion—it is working toward the single goal of production. It is a materialistic society, organised to produce things rather than people, with output set up as a god. Never before in history have social forces converged on so vast and so intensive a scale, but even the extent of the created wealth is less remarkable than the dynamic force of the human impulse that has brought this wealth into being.

Europe squanders her man-power and spares her substance, but America does exactly the reverse. For the past half-century, and especially during the last ten years, the Americans have been concentrating on the problem of obtaining the maximum efficiency of each worker. As a result of the use of machinery, of standardisation, and of intensive division and organisation of labour, productive methods have been renovated to a degree that few Europeans have ever dreamed of. In this super-collectivism, however, lies grave risk for the individual. His integrity is seriously threatened not only as a producer, but as a consumer as well.

If the aim of society is to produce the greatest amount of comfort and luxury for the greatest number of people, then the United States of America is in a fair way to succeed. And yet a house, a bath, and a car for every workman—so much luxury within the reach of all—can only be obtained at a tragic price, no less than the transformation of millions of workmen into automatons. 'Fordism,' which is the essence of American industry, results in the standardisation of the workman himself. Artisanship, now out of date, has no place in the New World, but with it have disappeared certain conceptions of mankind which we in Europe consider the very basis of civilisation. To express his own personality through his creative efforts is the ambition of every Frenchman, but it is incompatible with mass production.

We must not imagine that thoughtful Americans are unaware of the peril which is threatening their manhood, but it is too much to expect them to sacrifice their machines; for they give production priority over everything else. Having refused to save the individuality of the factory worker, they shift their defence to other grounds. During the day the worker may only be a cog in the machine, they say; but in the evening at any rate he becomes a man once more. His leisure, his money, the very things which mass production puts at his disposal, these will restore to him the manhood and intellectual independence of which his highly organised work has deprived him. This change in the centre of gravity in the life of the individual marks an absolute revolution in the ideas on which society in Western Europe has been built up. Can it be possible that the personality of the individual can recover itself in consumption after being so crippled and weakened in production? Have not the very products, in the form in which they are turned out by the modern factory, lost their individuality as well?

One of the finest attainments of American democracy has been to give much the same things to her poorest and richest citizens alike. The banker has his Rolls-Royce and the workman has his Ford. The banker's wife has her Paquin gown, and the working-girl chooses a similar one from the enormous quantities produced after the minimum of delay. The same applies all through the list. This generalised comfort is possible, first, because production is concentrated on a limited number of models repeated *ad infinitum,* and secondly, because the public is willing to put up with it. Thus we are forced to conclude that the price that America pays for her undeniable material progress is the sacrifice of one aspect of civilisation. . . .

Once it is admitted that their conception of society is materialistic in spite of the idealism of its leaders, it is only logical that the doctrine of efficiency should become the central idea of the country. To-day in America no sacrifice is too great to be endured for this sacred principle. There is no possible escape. Big profits overshadow liberty in all its forms, and the exercise of intelligence is encouraged only if it fits in with this common aim. Any one who turns aside to dabble in research or dilettantism is regarded as almost mentally perverted. Hence a growing tendency to reduce all virtues to the primordial ideal of conformity.

This point of view is not imposed by the upper classes or the government, but by the great masses of the people themselves. In the universities the majority of students are satisfied if they memorise an array of ready-made facts, and they seek from their professors not culture but the fundamentals of a successful career. In nothing does America more resemble Germany than in this discipline of thought. It may lead to splendid material results, and it is undoubtedly a marvellous aid to economic achievement; but under it originality and individual talent, and often art and genius, rebel or are stifled.

An important transformation of society results from this concentration of energy on the one supreme object of mass production. The individual, having become a means rather than an end, accepts his *rôle* of cog in the immense machine without giving a passing thought to the effect on his personality. Religion, also enrolled in the movement, exalts production as an ideal akin to the mysticism of life and of human progress. The ideal of 'service' sanctifies this collaboration and its superb material rewards. Caught between the atrophied individual and the over-disciplined community, the family finds its field of action greatly restricted; for in the eyes of the apostles of efficiency, the family is regarded as a barrier impeding the current. Though the Catholic Church still defends it, believing it to be one of its strongholds, yet society as a whole no longer relies on the home for the early training of the nation. It is to the public schools, the churches, to the ten thousand Y.M.C.A.'s and other associations for education and reform, to the press, and even to publicity that they look instead for the education of the masses. They pay little heed to the need of preserving for the jaded individual either the refuge of the family circle or the relaxation of meditation and culture. On the contrary, they consider them as obstacles in the way of progress. In the absence of an intermediate type of social institution in which co-operation is moderated by freedom, American society tends to adopt an aspect of practical collectivism. This collectivism is approved of by the upper classes and is whole-heartedly accepted by the masses; but it is subtly undermining the liberty of the individual and restricting his outlook to such an extent that without so much as regretting or realising it, he himself assents to his own abnegation. In this respect the American community is closer to the ancient civilisations in which the individual belonged to the City-State than is the social fabric of Western Europe which has evolved from the Middle Ages and the French Revolution. . . .

Those who seem to suffer most under this discipline are the foreign-born of the upper classes, but certain mature Americans also protest against it. The youth of the country makes no objection, and there is no reaction of the individual against this moral tyranny. The nation is not individualistic in mentality, and it therefore accepts this collectivism as part of itself; and the régime really suits it. The material advantages are so great, the security so perfect, and the enthusiasm of collective action in accomplishing stupendous tasks so overwhelming, that in an almost mystical abandon, other considerations are neither heeded nor missed.

But can the individual possibly survive in such an atmosphere? In her enthusiasm to perfect her material success, has not America risked quenching the flame of individual liberty which Europe has always regarded as one of the chief treasures of civilisation? At the very moment that America is enjoying a state of prosperity such as the world has never known before, an impartial observer is forced to ask whether this unprecedented abundance of wealth will in the long run lead to a higher form of civilisation. Europe, where industrial mass production was initiated, hesitates, terrified by the logical consequences. Will she end by adopting them? On the contrary, are they not incompatible with the old-established civilisation which so expresses her personality? Some who are eager to rejuvenate industrial Europe look to America for inspiration and guidance; but others hold back, deeming the past superior and preferable. . . .

The chief contrast between Europe and America is not so much one of geography as a fundamental difference between two epochs in the history of mankind, each with its own conception of life. We have the contrast between industrial mass production which absorbs the individual for its material conquests, as against the individual considered not merely as a means of production and progress but as an independent ego. From this unusual aspect we perceive certain traits that are common to the psychology of both Europe and the Orient. So the discussion broadens until it becomes a dialogue, as it were, between Ford and Gandhi.

JOHN BUCHAN
THE MOST VARIEGATED PEOPLE ON EARTH

Many Americans, especially if they have visited countries that have been politically aligned against the United States, may have heard critics of their country insist that they love the Americans as people, that their critique is only directed against the country's political, economic and social system. For John Buchan, Lord Tweedsmuir (1875-1940) there was no such distinction: he liked the Americans as a people and he liked their country.

When Buchan wrote about "My America" in Pilgrim's Way: An Essay in Recollection *(Cambridge, Mass: Houghton Mifflin, 1940) he had been Governor-General of Canada since 1935 and had had ample opportunity to observe the southern neighbor at close hand. Before that he had represented the Scottish universities in Parliament, distinguished himself as an historian and biographer and authored a long series of popular adventure stories. The following views are taken from pp. 267-274 of* Pilgrim's Way. *Permission to reprint granted by The Estate of Lord Tweedsmuir and Hodder & Stoughton.*

America is, no doubt, a vast country, though it can be comfortably put inside Canada. But it is not in every part a country of wide horizons. Dwellers on the Blue Ridge, on the prairies, and on the western ranges may indeed live habitually with huge spaces of land and sky, but most of America, and some of its most famous parts, is pockety, snug and cosy, a sanctuary rather than a watch-tower. To people so domiciled its vastness must be like the mathematician's space-time, a concept apprehended by the mind and not a percept of the eye. 'The largeness of Nature and of this nation were monstrous without a corresponding largeness and generosity of the spirit of the citizen.' That is one of Walt Whitman's best-known sayings, but let us remember that the bigness of their country is for most Americans something to be learned and imaginatively understood, and not a natural deduction from cohabiting with physical immensities.

Racially they are the most variegated people on earth. The preponderance of the Anglo-Saxon stock disappeared in the Civil War. Look today at any list of names in a society or a profession and you will find that, except in the navy, the bulk are from the continent of Europe. In his day Matthew Arnold thought that the chief source of the strength of the American people lay in their homogeneity and the absence of sharply defined classes, which made revolution unthinkable. Other observers, like Henry James, have deplored the lack of such homogeneity and wished for their country the 'close and complete consciousness of the Scots.' (I pause to note that I cannot imagine a more nightmare conception. What would happen to the world if a hundred and thirty million Scotsmen, with their tight, compact nationalism, were living in the same country?) I am inclined to query the alleged absence of classes, for I have never been in any part of the United States where class distinctions did not hold. There is an easy friendliness of manner which conceals a strong class pride, and the basis of that pride is not always, or oftenest, plutocratic. Apart from the social snobbery of the big cities, there seems to be everywhere an innocent love of grades and distinctions which is enough to make a communist weep. I have known places in the South where there was a magnificent aristocratic egalitarianism. Inside a charmed circle all were equal. The village postmistress, having had the right kind of great-great-grandmother, was an honoured member of society, while the immigrant millionaire, who had built himself a palace, might as well have been dead. And this is true not only of the New England F.F.M.'s and the Virginian F.F.V.'s, the districts with long traditions, but of the raw little townships in the Middle West. They, too, have their 'best' people who had ancestors, though the family tree may only have sprouted for two generations.

No country can show such a wide range of type and character, and I am so constituted that in nearly all I find something to interest and attract me. This is more than a temperamental bias, for I am very ready to give reasons for my liking. I am as much alive as anyone to the weak and ugly things in American life: areas, both urban and rural, where the human economy has gone rotten; the melting-pot which does not always melt; the eternal coloured problem; a constitutional machine which I cannot think adequately represents the efficient good sense of the American people; a brand of journalism which fatigues with its ruthless snappiness and uses a speech so disintegrated that it is incapable of expressing any serious thought or emotion; the imbecile patter of high-pressure salesmanship; an academic jargon, used chiefly by psychologists and sociologists, which is hideous and almost meaningless. Honest Americans do not deny these blemishes; indeed they are apt to exaggerate them, for they are by far the sternest critics of their own country. For myself, I would make a double plea in extenuation. These are defects from which today no nation is exempt, for they are the fruits of a mechanical civilisation, which perhaps are more patent in America, since everything there is on a large scale. Again, you can set an achievement very much the same in kind against nearly every failure. If her historic apparatus of government is cranky, she is capable of meeting the 'Instant need of things' with brilliant improvisations. Against economic plague-spots she can set great experiments in charity; against journalistic baby-talk a standard of popular writing in her best papers which is a model of idiom and perspicuity; against catch-penny trade methods many solidly founded, perfectly organised commercial enterprises; against the jargon of the half-educated professor much noble English prose in the great tradition. That is why it is so foolish to generalise about America. You no sooner construct a rule than it is shattered by the exceptions.

As I have said, I have a liking for almost every kind of American (except the kind who decry their country). I have even a sneaking fondness for George Babbitt, which I fancy is shared by his creator. But there are two types which I value especially, and which I have never met elsewhere in quite the same form. One is the pioneer. No doubt the physical frontier of the United States is now closed, but the pioneer still lives, though the day of the covered wagon is over. I have met him in the New England hills, where he is grave, sardonic, deliberate in speech; in the South, where he has a ready smile and a soft, caressing way of talking; in the ranges of the West, the cowpuncher with his gentle voice and his clear, friendly eyes which have not been dulled by reading print—the real thing, far removed from the vulgarities of film and fiction. At his best, I think, I have found him as a newcomer in Canada, where he is pushing north into districts like the Peace River, pioneering in the old sense. By what signs is he to be known? Principally by the fact that he is wholly secure, that he possesses his soul, that he is the true philosopher. He is one of the few aristocrats left in the world. He has a right sense of the values of life, because his cosmos embraces both nature and man. I think he is the most steadfast human being now alive.

The other type is at the opposite end of the social scale, the creature of a complex society who at the same time is not dominated by it, but, while reaping its benefits, stands a little aloof. In the older countries culture, as a rule, leaves some irregularity like an excrescence in a shapely tree-trunk, some irrational bias, some petulance or prejudice. You have to go to America, I think, for the wholly civilised man who has not lost his natural vigour or agreeable idiosyncrasies, but who sees life in its true proportions and has a fine balance of mind and spirit. It is a character hard to define, but anyone with a wide American acquaintance will know what I mean. They are people in whom education has not stunted any natural growth or fostered any abnormality. They are Greek in their justness of outlook, but Northern in their gusto. Their eyes are shrewd and candid, but always friendly. As examples I would cite, among friends who are dead, the names of Robert Bacon, Walter Page, Newton Baker, and Dwight Morrow.

But I am less concerned with special types than with the American people as a whole. Let me try to set down certain qualities which seem to me to flourish more lustily in the United States than elsewhere. Again, let me repeat, I speak of America only as I know it; an observer with different experience might not agree with my conclusions.

First I would select what, for want of a better word, I should call homeliness. It is significant that the ordinary dwelling, though it be only a shack in the woods, is called not a house, but a home. This means that the family, the ultimate social unit, is given its proper status as the foundation of society. It is often said that Americans are a nomad race, and it is true that they are very ready to shift their camp; but the camp, however bare, is always a home. The cohesion of the family is close, even when its members are scattered. This is due partly to the tradition of the first settlers, a handful in an unknown land; partly to the history of the frontier, where the hearth-fire burnt brighter when all around was cold and darkness. The later immigrants from Europe, feeling at last secure, were able for the first time to establish a family base, and they cherished it zealously. . . .

Second, I would choose the sincere and widespread friendliness of the people. Americans are interested in the human race, and in each other. Deriving doubtless from the old frontier days, there is a general helpfulness which I have not found in the same degree elsewhere. A homesteader in Dakota will accompany a traveller for miles to set him on the right road. The neighbours will rally round one of their number in distress with the loyalty of a Highland clan. This friendliness is not a self-conscious duty so much as an instinct. A squatter in a cabin will share his scanty provender and never dream that he is doing anything unusual.

American hospitality, long as I have enjoyed it, still leaves me breathless. The lavishness with which a busy man will give up precious time to entertain a stranger to whom he is in no way bound remains for me one of the wonders of the world. No doubt this friendliness, since it is an established custom, has its fake side. The endless brotherhoods and sodalities into which people brigade themselves encourage a geniality which is more a mannerism than an index of character, a tiresome, noisy, back-slapping heartiness. But that is the exception, not the rule. Americans like company, but though they are gregarious they do not lose themselves in the crowd. Waves of mass emotion may sweep the country, but they are transient things and do not submerge for long the stubborn rock of individualism. That is to say, people can be led, but they will not be driven. Their love of human companionship is based not on self-distrust, but on a genuine liking for their kind. With them the sense of a common humanity is a warm and constant instinct and not a doctrine of the schools or a slogan of the hustings.

Lastly—and this may seem a paradox—I maintain that they are fundamentally modest. Their interest in others is a proof of it; the Aristotelian Magnificent Man was interested in nobody but himself. As a nation they are said to be sensitive to criticism; that surely is modesty, for the truly arrogant care nothing for the opinion of other people. Above all they can laugh at themselves, which is not possible for the immodest. They are their own shrewdest and most ribald critics. It is charged against them that they are inclined to boast unduly about those achievements and about the greatness of their country, but a smug glorying in them is found only in the American of the caricaturist. They rejoice in showing their marvels to a visitor with the gusto of children exhibiting their toys to a stranger, an innocent desire, without any unfriendly gloating, to make others partakers in their satisfaction. If now and then they are guilty of bombast, it is surely a venial fault. The excited American talks of his land very much, I suspect, as the Elizabethans in their cups talked of England. The foreigner who strayed into the Mermaid Tavern must often have listened to heroics which upset his temper.

The native genius, in humour, and in many of the public and private relations of life, is for overstatement, a high-coloured, imaginative, paradoxical extravagance. The British gift is for understatement. Both are legitimate figures of speech. They serve the same purpose, for they call attention to a fact by startling the hearer, since manifestly they are not the plain truth. Personally I delight in both mannerisms and would not for the world have their possessors reject them. They serve the same purpose in another and a subtler sense, for they can be used to bring novel and terrible things within the pale of homely experience. I remember on the Western Front in 1918 that two divisions, British and American, aligned side by side, suffered a heavy shelling. An American sergeant described it in racy and imaginative speech which would have been appropriate to the Day of Judgment. A British sergeant merely observed that 'Kaiser 'ad been a bit 'asty.' Each had a twinkle in his eye; each in his national idiom was making frightfulness endurable by domesticating it.

ROBERT JUNGK
WORLD WITHOUT WALLS

Futurology, the study of what human life will be like in the future or, what we want it to be like, has moved beyond the speculative interest of a pioneer like H. G. Wells and is gradually gaining recognition as an established branch of the social sciences. Robert Jungk, who with Johan Galtung (see part VII, below) edited the significant symposium Mankind 2000 *(1969), is an influential contributor to the development of future research. When he warned that in the United States* Tomorrow Is Already Here, *however, he wrote within an established tradition including such diverse observers of the American scene as de Tocqueville, H. G. Wells and Georges Duhamel.*

Like Duhamel, Jungk obviously regarded certain trends in American society as a "menace", yet, as Herbert Agar remarks in his introduction to the British edition of Tomorrow Is Already Here, *"it is not solely the United States which is herein portrayed and lamented. The author is attacking a deformity of the whole western world—the materialism which, if continued, must dehumanize us." The following passages come from* Tomorrow Is Already Here: Scenes from a Man-Made World, *translated by Marguerite Waldman (London: Rupert*

Hart-Davis, 1954), pp. 188-196, 201-202.
Robert Jungk, Tomorrow Is Already Here © *by Scherz Verlag Bern-München-Wien. Reprinted by permission of Scherz Verlag and Granada Publishing Limited.*

An editor of *Ammunition,* a magazine published by the International Union of Automobile Workers, made the sharpest criticism I have yet heard of certain aspects of industrial psychology. He said to me: "During the war a 'soul engineer' in a factory whose men we organize asked them whom they hated most. At that time our adversaries naturally came first. If that man were to put the question today he would probably find that the leader in such an unpopularity contest was himself; the 'deep psychology' with which the human relations programmes are honouring us has become simply a new name for spying, a new way of driving and oppressing."

This prejudice is by no means universal. Many trade unionists are entirely in sympathy with the efforts of the industrial psychologists. They take exception only when the new techniques of soul-cure are misused. But that, they say, unfortunately occurs too often.

Perhaps a more eloquent complaint was one I heard from a man at the employing end, Mr L., the personnel chief of a motor parts factory. "Some of the things you'll see in my department will astonish and perhaps alarm you. They do me too." These were his surprising words when I handed him my letter of introduction from a close friend of his.

"I am not altogether blameless myself," he admitted. "It was I who first brought these Messrs 'Soul bunglers' and their assistants into the works. I had a great respect for science and hoped to accomplish something genuinely helpful to our people. But what came of it? A sniffing round and an agitation, a silly fooling with questionnaires, statistics and dozens of tests. And in return there's not a trace of healthy human understanding left. On paper the production in our factory seems to have risen through these methods. Despite the figures, I doubt it. But even if it were so, the price we pay is too high. Our factory has become a world without walls, without respect for individuality, without regard for private life. Why don't I draw the conclusion and leave? You ought to be able to figure that out without much psychology. I'm over fifty."

With these words Mr L. sent me to Mr H., who, although he nominally works under the chief who views the new methods with horror, has in actual fact the final say in the personnel department. H., a man of about forty, has the smooth porcelain face and courteous manners of the intelligent middle-grade general staff officer, a type one comes across on sub-committees of the Joint Chiefs of Staff in Washington.

H., as he told me, discovered his calling to personnel management when he was in the army. Driven more or less by chance into a department that used psychological tests to discover the particular aptitudes of recruits and placed them accordingly, he became, when the war was over, a specialist in choice and guidance of personnel.

Even at first glance his office resembles a laboratory. The walls are papered with coloured charts, complicated statistical exhibits and graphic curves which look like illustrations of the quantum theory. In these psychographs, productometers, motive profiles, sociograms and communication charts each worker appears as a fractional number—a decimal part of a total sum.

"The great new development in our field," affirms Mr H., "is the inclusion of the complete personality of the employee in our evaluations. The theory and practice of scientific management have made considerable strides in the past fifteen years. Former tests contented themselves with noting the surface aspects of the candidate, such as mental reaction and signs of physical skill. Today with the help of personality tests we try to look deeper into the motives of our people. How is their emotional stability? Are they honest? Are they loyal? Do they get on with their fellow-workers? What is the state of their private life? Are they married? Have they sex problems? Do they spend their money easily? What is their relationship with their parents? What with their children? Have they got inhibitions? Are they aggressive?

"Each of our employees is appraised according to forty personality traits, beginning with his upbringing, continuing through his capacity for remembering names, on to his political orientation. We don't, of course, wish to exert any direct influence on his political opinions, but as an expression of his personality these, too, seem implicitly important and informative."

"These tests must be very long and expensive," I interposed.

Mr H. was not of that opinion. Actually, he said, they saved the firm substantial sums. To put the wrong man in the wrong place, to give responsibility to a person incapable of taking it—these were the things that really cost money. According to his own calculations—he had splendidly illustrated memoranda on the subject to show me—the firm had saved 14.3 per cent in the past year on repairs alone because more carefully chosen people operated the machines. "A single workman can cost us thousands of dollars in damages through a mistake in the handling of a valuable machine. We invest two thousand dollars' worth of instruction in each new worker and see no point in losing it simply because we haven't adequately tested the man's character before engaging him. One single foreman who lets his childish aggressions react on the workers under him can release all sorts of protest responses, which then appear in the form of five-figure losses in the production statistics."

H. proudly showed me the interview rooms in which people seeking jobs were interrogated, given forms to fill in or watched by a tester for their reactions to certain psychological tables. With naïve pride he showed me the files kept in connection with everyone holding or aspiring to a post. There was the information of a local credit office regarding his financial circumstances, reports of his teachers and former chiefs, reports of a detective agency about his private life.

"We leave nothing to chance," said Mr H., "and we've been proved right.". . .

Advocates of industrial psychology can produce a number of strong arguments for increased psychological penetration of the working world. They believe that the advantages to be gained by probing deeply into personality and private life far outweigh the disadvantages. The people who are tested, they say, are themselves generally grateful for having been prevented from taking up posts they would have been unable to fill. At the same time the continual observation of all employees makes possible the speedier advancement of many a gifted person who would formerly have remained unnoticed.

But in practice many cases contradict this friendly picture. Since it is a matter of mass choice the tests are apt to be applied hurriedly, superficially and mechanically. Only too often distorted results are produced and the fate of a capable person endangered by the faulty inferences of a soul engineer with too much work piled on his desk.

Despite such errors, which no one denies, American industry keeps to its new system of psychological choice and guidance because, as the personnel chief of a California aeroplane factory told me, there is no other feasible standard for allotting posts.

"What could we go by otherwise?" he asked. "Hundreds of people about whom we know nothing come into my department in the course of a month asking for employment. When the factories were small and the job-seekers came chiefly from the neighbourhood it was easy to dispense with tests. One knew their neighbours, friends, teachers, former employers. But nowadays people travel thousands of miles to find work in a region that suits them. Look at today's application list alone: a man from Vermont, another from Arkansas, a third from Chicago, a fourth from Portland. We can't, really, rely altogether on their word."

An assiduous young psychologist in General Motors who looks after about two hundred thousand people defended the system as follows: "Our concerns have grown to such dimensions that the relationship between the upper and middle ranks and the mass of workers has naturally become less familiar than formerly. In a little business of about a hundred men the chief used to know his people and the people knew each other fairly well. It was easy then to find out which people deserved advancement or a rise in wages. The psychological test is unhappily a necessary substitute for years of close acquaintance. Now we are obliged to conduct mass interrogations regularly, if only to be able to ascertain the general mood in the works."

One of the main difficulties in the way of a fair application of psychological tests is the scarcity of trained psychologists. In 1950, when thousands of firms were demanding the help of soul engineers, there were only three hundred qualified industrial psychologists in existence. Therefore only the largest firms can, for the present, maintain house psychologists. The others must have recourse to special concerns, such as the Psychological Corporation of New York, thoroughly serious firms, in the midst of the many spurious ones that have followed the trend and plunged into the tempting business of soul guidance.

The fees demanded by the psychological advisory firms are high. They are generally consulted, for the first time, when strong signs of social unrest appear in some part of a factory organism. A sudden fall in the production figures not to be accounted for by technical deficiencies, an unusual accumulation of defective products, quarrels in one or more departments and threats of strike are usually the occasion.

The Psychological Corporation, when the alarm is given, moves in at once with its specialists and the whole bag of tricks for the investigation of psychological unrest. The inevitable questionnaires are distributed, personal interviews held with the staff of the business from top to bottom, and on occasion, if simple methods prove inadequate, microphones concealed here and there for the reception of "candid reactions"—that is, expressions of the employees not intended for the ears of the observers.

The diagnosis reached through the investigation, if the business is very large, is obtained by the collation of the facts according to a definite system, stamping on perforated cards and calculations of the average value. The ostensible mood can then be exactly stated in percentages. . . .

When a firm of psychological advisers has made its report and pointed out ways to a psychological cure, it does not fail to recommend regular difficulties and to offer its own services in this respect at a reduced subscription price.

Such a service comprises a test programme to eliminate from the start all possible trouble-makers and failures among the prospective employees; secondly comes a "merit rating" programme which again scrutinizes the employees and establishes their capacities at regular intervals, considering whether a man is under or over paid, whether he ought to be dismissed or promoted; finally, a "morale-building" programme, which is responsible for the maintenance of a good mood and working spirit in the business. . . .

The technique of the group interview is practised with considerable success. Eight or ten candidates for employment or promotion are brought together in the same room. They are given a general discussion theme closely connected with their work—in an aeroplane concern for example "The advantages and disadvantages of air freight traffic"—and left to themselves for a prearranged period of generally about an hour. But only in appearance, for at least three observers belonging to the advisory firm are listening to the debates, and marking each candidate according to various criteria: Is he too aggressive?

Is he too passive? Is he convincing? Amiable? Does he have personal magnetism? Capacities of leadership? Is he patient or does he easily become irritable?

"The ideal arrangement for such a group interview", writes Harold Fields, one of the testers in the employ of the city of New York, "is a room in which the candidates sit around a table. The walls are of glass, transparent from the outside and like a mirror on the inside. Behind them sits the invisible testing committee. Openings in the wall make it possible to hear what is being said in the room."

The so-called self-valuation techniques have also begun to find favour. Employees who work in the same group are provided with questionnaires in which they are requested to state in confidence to the soul engineer their opinion of their nearest fellow-worker. In this way the psychological examiner is said to obtain an exact picture of the "social build-up of the group". He can then, for example, remove a particular harmful element from this body and introduce instead an active optimistic element.

While the participants in such interviews at least know that they are being watched and appraised, this is not true in the case of many of the newer psychological screenings. Sales personnel in department stores and shops are regularly examined for their abilities by testers of the Willmark Corporation who pose as customers. These investigators, to make the deception complete, go to the length of purchasing wares which are later returned to the firm. A report on each sales person is prepared on a form, stating among other things whether he has been friendly or sullen, whether he tried, by suggestive sales-technique, to encourage the customer to buy more, whether he kept the disciplinary rules of the business, how he took leave of the customer. It is a matter of pride with the Willmark Service System and its thirty-three branches all over America that virtually none of its sales analysts is ever unmasked by one of his victims.

Some firms use the system of keeping an applicant waiting at length in an ante-room while they have him watched through television cameras or simply by a schooled secretary. Before the man has even had a chance to speak with the chief of personnel he has been unwittingly judged and condemned. For they believe it possible to determine by the degree of friendliness with which he greets the secretary, the assurance with which he expresses his wish, the calm or nervousness with which he waits, whether he uses his time to read the magazines at his disposal or to look ahead of him in boredom, trepidation or annoyance, whether he is suitable for the vacant post.

The American partiality for mechanical patents has created a large series of machines for judging and assessing human beings. Tape-recording instruments, television equipment, cameras and complicated calculating machines are introduced. The chronograph, invented by the anthropologist, Eliot Chaple, is said to be able to measure the initiative, skill, friendliness and other qualities of the good salesman with ninety-per-cent exactitude.

But the most uncanny of the machines is the polygraph, now employed by at least three hundred American firms and popularly called the lie-detector. When it became known that this apparatus had been installed by important government offices of national defence, for use in the selection of their personnel, a storm was raised in the press against such a violation of the rights of personal freedom. This practice is said to have then been abandoned. But the business world was untouched by the wave of protest, and there the polygraph is used more and more.

At first the lie-detector was employed only by the police for the purpose of obtaining confessions. Then the private detective agencies added polygraph departments in order to be able to offer their clients this new service. Banks, insurance companies and similar types of enterprise in which there was danger of embezzlement began to make use of the new apparatus with great success. Department stores and chain stores followed suit. They started the practice of sending their employees every three months for a polygraph test, on the correct assumption that fear of such an examination would eliminate or sub-stantially reduce the small thefts from the stockrooms customary in such businesses. When the armaments industry was obliged to conceal more and more of its work the trial by lie-detector was made a pre-requisite to the engagement of any person whose function it would be to deal with confidential orders of the armed forces. . . .

Certainly the use of the lie-detector for personnel selection repre-sents the limit of the psychotechnical invasion of personality and it would be unfair to judge all the accomplishments of industrial psychology by the exaggerations for which it is responsible.

But even the far more innocent and ethically unobjectionable techniques of counselling, the public opinion polls and the promotion of happy industrial relations, have indirect effects all too reminiscent of similar phenomena in the totalitarian states. Knowing that before and during their employment they are being watched by people in whose hands lie their economic fate, many who wish to keep their jobs speak in a way that does not reflect their true feelings.

Millions of Americans, as soon as they cross the threshold of their place of work step, partly consciously, partly almost unconsciously, into roles which correspond to what the soul engineers expect of them. They are happy, and "keep smiling" even when they do not feel so inclined. They act as though they were "well balanced" and "perfectly normal" even when they have a tremendous urge to kick over the traces. They strain every fibre to suppress their natural aggressiveness and to be "good companions" with whom everyone easily gets along, even when they would like to break into loud curses at the man at the next desk. And above all they behave as though they were loyal to the firm through thick and thin, even if they find more to criticize in it than to praise.

This standard mask of the "jolly good fellow", of the "easy-going guy", of the "sweet girl", grows on to some of them as a second face. It is no longer a question of the inner conscience, of a true impulse of the soul, but of codes of behaviour coming from the outside. To judge how the wind from the heights of the directors' offices will blow, how the potential giver of an order would like the salesman to behave, to guess how a superior pictures the man whom he will promote, this is the most important asset in the battle for a living. In places of rules and regulations imposed by the authorities appears a far stricter self-censorship. Be sure to do nothing striking or unusual, which could be regarded as neurotic, as egotistical, as maladjusted or perhaps even revolutionary.

Thus in the "world without walls" which has increasingly come to be, the type of man on which America's greatness was based is becoming rarer and rarer: the strong, free man guided by his own conscience, constantly searching for something new. Since four out of five Americans today are employees (as against one in five a hundred years ago), a profound alteration in the national character is taking place, a contradiction of the democratic tradition and a cause of concern to every friend of America.

M. STURUA
BIG BROTHER IS WATCHING YOU

Is the United States a police state? Considering its source, the accusation in this article from Izvestia *in 1969 may strike some readers as audacious. However, rather than allow ourselves to become involved in a discussion of the "I-am-better-than-you-are" variety we should consider the facts and views of M. Sturua on their own merits and ponder the question: How free is our so-called free world society?*

Sturua's central image of contemporary America is the anti-Utopia of George Orwell's novel 1984. *Orwell, who remained a revolutionary (but independent) socialist, hardly "thought he was painting the socialist future" in this book. In fact it is ironic that a Soviet writer should find it necessary to thus characterize a novel that is an attack on totalitarianism of any color and that draws as much upon tendencies Orwell had observed in his own society and in the fascist regimes as upon the Soviet Union under Stalin.*

The following excerpt from "What the U.S.A. Is Like: The Sullen Eagle," Izvestia *Sept. 10, 1969, is taken from the translation in* The Current Digest of the Soviet Press, *XXI, no. 37 (Oct. 8, 1969), pp. 18-19.*

Translation copyright 1974 by The Current Digest of the Soviet Press, *published weekly at the Ohio State University by the American Association for the Advancement of Slavic Studies; reprinted by permission of the Digest.*

New York, September— . . . The new school year has begun in the schools of America. As long ago as 1954, the U.S. Supreme Court with great pomp declared the unconstitutionality of segregation in education. In fifteen years only a third of the schools have become "biracial." This year the government has bowed to the racists. Mr. Finch, Secretary of Health, Education and Welfare, has announced that "rapid execution of desegregation plans will result in chaos and catastrophe." But why do you say "rapid," Mr. Finch; after all, it's not the sixteenth year?! . . .

Political circles in Washington make no secret of the fact that a deal has been concluded between the racists and the Administration.

Taking advantage of the fact that the fate of Safeguard [antiballistic missile legislation] hung by a thread, Senators on the right began cynically to blackmail the Administration. In the words of The New York Times, "the President, Attorney General Mitchell and Secretary Finch yielded to pressure from John Stennis, the Senator from Mississippi."

It is a scene worthy of the gods: In order to saddle the country with new military burdens, with a new threat of atomic apocalypse, the Republican Administration has sacrificed the democratic rights of white Americans and the hopes of non-white Americans for equality. But we should not pity Washington for its being blackmailed by the rightists. Its readiness to give way to the extortionists was suspiciously hasty.

Some time ago the Englishmen George Orwell, one of the most vicious haters of communism, wrote a pamphleteering novel "1984." In describing "Big Brother," a fantastic symbol of total surveillance, who keeps watch on everyone and everything with an ever-vigilant television eye, Orwell thought he was painting the socialist future. But it turns out that "1984" is nothing less than a report on life under capitalism, and the report is anything but fantastic.

"The New York City Police Department has set up a 'War Room,' which is equipped with electronic apparatus, in order to keep all assemblages, especially parades and demonstrations, under constant surveillance *** The 'War Room,' windowless, is situated on the third floor of New York City Police Headquarters. From it officers on duty keep watch on gatherings, either by means of stationary television cameras set up in such places as Times Square, City Hall Park or the square in front of the U.N. Building, or by portable television equipment in helicopters that patrol the city*** The 'War Room' is dominated by three enormous screens—one measuring 13 feet by 10 feet, and two 10 feet by 7 feet." None of this is from Orwell's book. This is from the news columns of The New York Times. And the year is 1969, not 1984.

New York is not an exception. During this "cool summer" in Washington, underneath the Pentagon parking lot a so-called "operations center" was opened. There, an army headquarters for "controlling crisis situations" was installed. It is totally unrelated to international conflict. Its concern is civil war. To enter the "operations center" is to find yourself in a world of science fiction. All around is electronic computer equipment, and, feeding it, a "memory bank" containing 130,000,000 items of every kind of information; there are flashing screens, maps that light up, glassed-in "observation balconies" and a network of communications branching out in all directions.

The "operations center" in the catacombs of the Pentagon is linked to 150 major cities in America, which were chosen on the basis of a "cybernetic study of centers of disorders." The center can simultaneously observe disorders in 25 different locations in the United States. It has at its disposal two army brigades with 3,000 men in each—one for the West Coast and the other for the East Coast. These "fire-fighting brigades" possess extraordinary mobility and can be dispatched to the center of a crisis on very short notice.

And in the glassed-in "observation balconies" sit the only dispatchers of their kind. Examining the data from the cybernetic machines, they are whispering, raising their eyes to the screens, "Thank God, it's over!"

Is it over? The Director of the F.B.I., the familiar Edgar Hoover, mentally shuddering, has held forth at length in his department's monthly Bulletin on the anarchist threat to the nation. Anarchy? Really? To challenge the authorities has become the everyday norm in the United States; the footsteps are drawing nearer. The authorities are nervously awaiting the start of the new school year in the universities. Several student organizations are planning mass antiwar demonstrations throughout the country, including the usual march on Washington. And so the "operations center" in the Pentagon will soon receive its baptism by fire. The footsteps draw nearer. Hoover is particularly upset by the decision of the young people of revolutionary inclination to transfer their center of concern from university grounds to the factories and by the fact that throughout the country militant pacts are being made between radical student groups and Negro organizations. . . .

IV. THE BUSINESS OF GOVERNMENT

American democracy has long been an inspiration and a model for progressives and revolutionaries the world over since the time of the signing of its two cornerstones: the Declaration of Independence and the Constitution. A telling example of how the United States has continued to be a source of inspiration for independence movements is the sentence with which Ho Chi Minh chose to open the Vietnamese Declaration of Independence: "All men are created equal; they are endowed by the creator with certain unalienable Rights; among these are Life, Liberty and the Pursuit of Happiness." However, as democratic institutions have become more wide-spread and observers are less easily impressed by regular popular elections and other outward forms of democracy, critical analyses of the way the people of the United States are governed have proliferated. The four observers whose comments are presented below are all concerned with different aspects of the common man's lack of influence on government.

Why did American politics develop into a "business?" What are the consequences of such a "spoils system?" What effective role does the individual have in the political system? Why is the participation of American citizens in the affairs of their government so low? Is there a reasonable prospect that this participation will improve? What might serve to forestall any improvement? Why is "more government" the American answer to all Social problems? To what extent is the business of American Government business? What does that mean for the individual citizen? Why are businessmen more respected in America than intellectuals?

MAX WEBER
THE SPOILS SYSTEM

While all may not agree with the outstanding German sociologist Max Weber's (1864-1920) characterization of the two major American political parties as "purely organizations of job hunters drafting their changing platforms according to the chances of vote-grabbing," few would insist that they are parties with a clear ideological or class base like those found in Europe. Party politics in the United States is in many respects a business, a profession more than a means of setting certain sets of ideas into action. Although the difference between the United States and European democracies may not be too great in practice, there is a significant difference in the underlying assumptions and principles. Some differences, however, may still be easily appreciated. In Scandinavian countries, for example, there is a sizable contingent of industrial workers, farmers, and fishermen in parliament, people who do not regard themselves as "professional politicians" and who later may return to their original vocations. In comparison, how many American Congressmen are on temporary leave from the assembly line?

Max Weber's "Politics as a Vocation" was first given as a lecture in 1918. The following version is taken from H. H. Gerth and C. Wright Mius' translation and edition, From Max Weber: Essays in Sociology (London: Routledge & Kegan Lane, 1948), edited and translated by H. H. Gerth and C. Wright Mills. Copyright 1946 by Oxford University Press, Inc. Reprinted by permission. pp. 107-111.

According to Washington's idea, America was to be a commonwealth administered by 'gentlemen.' In his time, in America, a gentleman was also a landlord, or a man with a college education—this was the case at first. In the beginning, when parties began to organize, the members of the House of Representatives claimed to be leaders, just as in England at the time when notables ruled. The party organization was quite loose and continued to be until 1824. In some communities, where modern development first took place, the party machine was in the making even before the eighteen-twenties. But when Andrew Jackson was first elected President—the election of the western farmers' candidate—the old traditions were overthrown. For-

mal party leadership by leading members of Congress came to an end
soon after 1840, when the great parliamentarians, Calhoun and Web-
ster, retired from political life because Congress had lost almost all
of its power to the party machine in the open country. That the plebiscitarian 'machine' has developed so early in America is due to the
fact that there, and there alone, the executive—this is what mat-
tered—the chief of office-patronage, was a President elected by plebis-
cite. By virtue of the 'separation of powers' he was almost independent of parliament in his conduct of office. Hence, as the price of
victory the true booty object of the office-prebend was held out precisely at the presidential election. Through Andrew Jackson the 'spoils
system' was quite systematically raised to a principle and the conclusions were drawn.

What does this spoils system, the turning over of federal offices
to the following of the victorious candidate, mean for the party forma-
tions of today? It means that quite unprincipled parties oppose one
another; they are purely organizations of job hunters drafting their
changing platforms according to the chances of vote-grabbing, changing their colors to a degree which, despite all analogies, is not yet
to be found elsewhere. The parties are simply and absolutely fashioned
for the election campaign that is most important for office patronage:
the fight for the presidency and for the governorships of the separate
states. Platforms and candidates are selected at the national conventions of the parties without intervention by congressmen. Hence they
emerge from party conventions, the delegates of which are formally,
very democratically elected. These delegates are determined by meet-
ings of other delegates, who, in turn, owe their mandate to the
'primaries,' the assembling of the direct voters of the party. In the
primaries the delegates are already elected in the name of the candidate
for the nation's leadership. Within the parties the most embittered fight
rages about the question of 'nomination.' After all, 300,000 to
400,000, official appointments lie in the hands of the President,
appointments which are executed by him only with the approval of
the senators from the separate states. Hence the senators are powerful
politicians. By comparison, however, the House of Representatives
is, politically, quite important because patronage of office is removed
from it and because the cabinet members, simply assistants to the President, can conduct office apart from the confidence or lack of confi-

dence of the people. The President, who is legitimatized by the people, confronts everybody, even Congress; this is a result of 'the separation of powers.'

In America, the spoils system, supported in this fashion, has been technically possible because American culture with its youth could afford purely dilettante management. With 300,000 to 400,000 such party men who have no qualifications to their credit other than the fact of having performed good services for their party, this state of affairs of course could not exist without enormous evils. A corruption and wastefulness second to none could be tolerated only by a country with as yet unlimited economic opportunities.

Now then, the boss is the figure who appears in the picture of this system of the plebiscitarian party machine. Who is the boss? He is a political capitalist entrepreneur who on his own account and at his own risk provides votes. He may have established his first relations as a lawyer or a saloonkeeper or as a proprietor of similar establishments, or perhaps as a creditor. From here he spins his threads out until he is able to 'control' a certain number of votes. When he has come this far he establishes contact with the neighboring bosses, and through zeal, skill, and above all discretion, he attracts the attention of those who have already further advanced in the career, and then he climbs. The boss is indispensable to the organization of the party and the organization is centralized in his hands. He substantially provides the financial means. How does he get them? Well, partly by the contributions of the members, and especially by taxing the salaries of those officials who came into office through him and his party. Furthermore, there are bribes and tips. He who wishes to trespass with impunity one of the many laws needs the boss's connivance and must pay for it; or else he will get into trouble. But this alone is not enough to accumulate the necessary capital for political enterprises. The boss is indispensable as the direct recipient of the money of great financial magnates, who would not entrust their money for election purposes to a paid party official, or to anyone else giving public account of his affairs. The boss, with his judicious discretion in financial matters, is the natural man for those capitalist circles who finance the election. The typical boss is an absolutely sober man. He does not seek social honor; the 'professional' is despised in 'respectable society.' He seeks power alone, power as a source of money, but also power for power's sake. In contrast to the English leader, the American boss works in the dark. He is not heard speaking in public; he suggests to the speakers what they must say in expedient fashion. He himself, however, keeps silent. As a rule he accepts no office, except that of senator. For, since the senators, by virtue of the Constitution, participate in office patronage, the leading bosses often sit in person in this body. The distribution of offices is carried out, in the first place, according to services done for the party. But, also, auctioning offices on financial bids often occurs and there are certain rates for individual offices; hence, a system of selling offices exists which, after all, has often been known also to the monarchies, the church-state included, of the seventeenth and eighteenth centuries.

The boss has no firm political 'principles'; he is completely unprincipled in attitude and asks merely: What will capture votes? Frequently he is a rather poorly educated man. But as a rule he leads an inoffensive and correct private life. In his political morals, however, he naturally adjusts to the average ethical standards of political conduct, as a great many of us also may have done during the hoarding period in the field of economic ethics. That as a 'professional' politician the boss is socially despised does not worry him. That he personally does not attain high federal offices, and does not wish to do so, has the frequent advantage that extra-party intellects, thus notables, may come into candidacy when the bosses believe they will have great appeal value at the polls. Hence the same old party notables do not run again and again, as is the case in Germany. Thus the structure of these unprincipled parties with their socially despised power-holders has aided able men to attain the presidency—men who with us never would have come to the top. To be sure, the bosses resist an outsider who might jeopardize their sources of money and power. Yet in the competitive struggle to win the favor of the voters, the bosses frequently have had to condescend and accept candidates known to be opponents of corruption.

Thus there exists a strong capitalist party machine, strictly and thoroughly organized from top to bottom, and supported by clubs of extraordinary stability. These clubs, such as Tammany Hall, are like Knight orders. They seek profits solely through political control, especially of the municipal government, which is the most important object of booty. This structure of party life was made possible by the high degree of democracy in the United States—a 'New Country.' This connection, in turn, is the basis for the fact that the system is gradually dying out. America can no longer be governed only by dilettantes. Scarcely fifteen years ago, when American workers were asked why they allowed themselves to be governed by politicians whom they admitted they despised, the answer was: 'We prefer having people in office whom we can spit upon, rather than a caste of officials who spit upon us, as is the case with you.' This was the old point of view of American 'democracy.' Even then, the socialists had entirely different ideas and now the situation is no longer bearable. The dilettante administration does not suffice and the Civil Service Reform establishes an ever-increasing number of positions for life with pension rights. The reform works out in such a way that university-trained officials, just as incorruptible and quite as capable as our officials, get into office. Even now about 100,000 offices have ceased being objects of booty to be turned over after elections. Rather, the offices qualify their holders for pensions, and are based upon tested qualifications. The spoils system will thus gradually recede into the background and the nature of party leadership is then likely to be transformed also—but as yet, we do not know in what way.

GUNNAR MYRDAL
THE SPECIAL CASE OF THE UNITED STATES

Lecturing in 1918, Max Weber predicted the demise of the spoils system without venturing any guesses on what effects this would have on the party system. Forty years later, in his series of lectures on "Economic Planning in the Welfare States and its International Implications" at Yale University, the Swedish economist and statesman Gunnar Myrdal (1898-   ) saw the low level of active popular participation in politics in the United States as a "special case" and tried to "explain why such a large proportion of counties and towns are inefficiently governed, [and] why they have sometimes lapsed into corrupted boss rule."

When Myrdal claims that his optimistic view of the future of democracy in the United States is "realistic" he has a more solid foundation for his claim than most foreign observers. The monumental work of

his many years as a close student of American society is An American
Dilemma *(1944), the controversial but still most comprehensive explo-
ration of what was then called the Negro problem.*

*Myrdal's comments on American politics and the future of the
democratic welfare states are taken from* Beyond the Welfare State
*(London: Gerald Duckworth & Co., 1960), pp. 38-40, 72-74.
Copyright © 1960 by Yale University Press.*

The Welfare State has to devote continual vigilance to the building
up and preservation of its human basis in democratic participation on
the part of the people. In the countries where this problem has been
tackled most seriously, and which also, on the whole, have been most
successful in their strivings to keep up and widen active popular participation, a widely diversified educational campaign is continually
carried on by the organisations and the political parties. They equip
themselves with research facilities, they have specialised organisations
for young people and for women, they run publishing houses, they
issue papers and periodicals, print pamphlets and books, they set up
training schools of their own and organise local study groups and discussion circles, etc. They correspond intensively with their members,
and are sometimes prepared to make considerable sacrifices in managerial efficiency by putting up important decisions to membership
referendum.

As regards active participation, the situation varies considerably as
between the several Western countries. Generally speaking, it is still
rather low in the United States. The explanations usually offered for
this deficiency in the American national community are not very convincing. One such popular explanation is the size of the country. That
the country is big does not explain, however, why the percentage of
the electorate voting in elections, national or local, is relatively so
small. Neither does it explain why such a large proportion of counties
and towns are inefficiently governed, nor why they have sometimes
lapsed into currupted boss rule.

Another popular explanation is that the country is still so young.
This is a statement of doubtful validity in the present context. The
United States, in fact, is the oldest modern democracy; its trade union
movement, for example, is several generations older than that of the
Scandinavian countries, where it has reached so much higher levels

of efficiency and democratic control. A scrutiny of the facts in the United States itself, as well as a comparison of the facts in the several Western countries, does not reveal any positive correlation between the age of an institutional pattern of cooperation and bargaining and the degree of effective popular participation and control. If anything, we observe rather that the malaise of non-participation is particularly prevalent in many of the organisations in America which carry their records furthest back, and in some of the national communities in the rest of the Western world—as England and Australia—which were once pioneers in building up the organisational state.

The observation that people in America move around more frequently and over a wider area does not by itself explain the lower level of popular participation and the consequent failings in efficiency and honesty in local and sectional self-rule. Historically, among many other concomitant social changes accounted for in Chapter 3, it was, in Europe, precisely the intensified internal migrations following industrialisation that ultimately resulted in the coming into being of closely integrated national communities. These naturally had an even more intensified civic activity also in the organisations for provincial and municipal self-government—though this development occasionally led through periods of maladjustment related to the migrations. On balance and in the longer run, the high mobility in America is the surest basis of hope for a more closely-knit national community with more intensive popular participation in civic life on all levels. And, as a matter of fact, deficiencies in these respects have consistently been most glaring in those pockets of the American national communities which have been relatively isolated and stagnant and where mobility has been low.

As neither size and youth, nor mobility, by themselves, afford a satisfactory explanation for the relative imperfections in democratic participation on all levels in the United States, I believe that instead we must relate them to the fact that the country, until comparatively recently, has had much immigration, which in its later stages brought in people from national cultures rather different from the older stock. In spite of the very rapid advances made towards national integration, heterogeneous elements still linger everywhere in the population, and with them remnants of separatistic allegiances.

This line of explanation should make us optimistic in regard to the future development of the democratic organisational state in the United States. As the development towards national integration proceeds, it should be fairly safe to assume that the intensity of active participation by the Americans in their organisations and their other communities, from local to national level, will rise. No one who has watched America over a couple of decades can remain unaware of the tremendous improvement in this respect, and of the consequent rise in efficiency, democratic control, and honesty, particularly in the private power groups and the authorities for provincial and municipal self-government, where the deficiencies were biggest and are still rather considerable.

This problem of citizens' participation is of the utmost importance, not only in America but everywhere in the Western countries, and should be made the subject of intensive study. I am aware that, to a varying degree in the several countries, the Welfare State is, as yet, more of a hope and an appearance than a reality. In some countries and in some fields it is indeed very imperfect. . . .

Nevertheless, I persist in my optimism which in this case I believe is realistic. What is possible—what is accomplished here and there, and what we see glimmering everywhere—has reality as a goal which can be reached and, indeed, must be reached, if democracy shall not lose its chance. I trust that, once people are free to organise for cooperation and bargaining, and once they also have got equal say in determining state policy which sets the conditions for this cooperation and bargaining, they will not for long tolerate such deficiencies. I cannot believe that, when the people have become sovereign, they will choose to leave their Welfare State as that rather shallow, bureaucratic, strongly centralised, institutional machinery, manipulated by crafty and powerful private operators and vested interests, which it is doomed to become, if it is not vitalised by citizens' participation to an ever higher degree. . . .

The process by which local self-government and a balanced and effective infra-structure of open and democratically controlled organisations are coming into their own is in none of the Western countries carried to completion; in some countries it sometimes seems as if this process of decentralisation of government is reversed, at least temporarily and in some fields. To build up and preserve popular participation in government at all levels is everywhere an acute problem.

Education in the operation of grass-root democracy and solidarity with the community have nowhere reached such high levels that informal community controls have acquired anything like their maximum effectiveness. It is against this background we have to understand the tendency of the reformers everywhere to look for more direct state intervention as the means of improving the life of their national communities.

For various reasons, these persistent weaknesses in the very foundation of the Welfare State are much more pronounced in the United States. There, as I mentioned in Chapter 4, popular participation is comparatively low on all levels. As a consequence of this, local and sectional cooperation and bargaining is relatively ineffective in the face of the vested interests, and sometimes infected by machine and boss rule and by corruption. The process of national integration has still a considerable distance to go before identification, solidarity and participation reach the levels common in the other Western countries. This is so, not because the American nation is big and has so much space to live in, nor because it is young, nor because the people in America are so mobile, but because it still bears the impact of being composed of the descendants of immigrants with different cultural backgrounds who show separatistic loyalties.

Not unrelated to this, the United States has also more than its due share of a structure of social relations that is still legalistic. It depends more on rigid state regulations and has an overgrown bureaucracy with, relatively speaking, not very high standards of efficiency and economy of effort. When the Americans are ahead of all the other Western nations in productivity, it is accomplished in spite of these shortcomings in their public life, and has to be explained in terms of the rich natural resources in their spacious realm and the spectacularly efficient organisation of private business: the work on the farms, in the factories, in the shops and in the offices.

With their lingering heterogeneity and separatistic loyalties, the Americans undoubtedly need far more state legislation to lay down general rules for conduct in life and work than the more homogeneous nations do. And as local and sectional community control is weaker and often less in line with the ideals of the national community, there are many more fields of social life in the United States where there is need for direct state control through the courts and the administration in order to enforce those general mores. This also explains why we find that in the United States further centralization of controls is so much the policy of those who seek to promote progress. It explains why the politicians and the ordinary citizens, irrespective of the political party they belong to, so regularly think of direct state intervention as the appropriate remedy for wrongs. In no other country does the thought that "there ought to be a law against" this or that so readily come up in every discussion about conditions in the national community.

It is important, however, not least in the United States, to keep in mind as a long-range goal the values in decentralising the community controls. As I see it, the strivings towards that goal are not hopeless. Even in America the conditions are gradually being created for more efficient collective authorities on the local and sectional levels. The rapid national integration in America can also, I believe, be relied upon to gradually decrease that country's special need of laying down general rules by legislation and of having to rely upon central state controls in order to enforce their observance. And the reformers in America have reason to remember that in this process the communities and organisations beneath the state level are apt to increase more rapidly in effectiveness and active participation of the people, the more scope they are given. For this reason it is rational to take risks, and even to make temporary sacrifices, in the endeavour to spread out ever wider and deeper the roots of democracy in the national community. This is indeed the meaning of the old and cherished American saying that the remedy of what is still imperfect and wrong in society is more, and ever more, democracy.

A rather important fact is that people in American as in other Western countries dislike a meddlesome state, regimentation and red tape. It is true, as I have stressed, that there is a growing satisfaction among ordinary people in all our countries with the relative levels of abundance, equality and security which we are reaching. I even pointed to the emergence of a "created harmony" of interests in the Welfare State. It is also true that people become accustomed to a regulated life when that has become the set pattern. They accept that life more willingly, however, when they themselves participate in making and managing the regulations that govern them.

There is now, in all our countries, a rising tide of resentment against tinkering by the state organs, which sometimes detracts from the appreciation of the Welfare State as such. As we are still in the transitional stage, when the volume of direct state intervention is continually rising, because national planning has not caught up with the need for coordination and simplification and because cooperation and bargaining in the collective organisations beneath the state level have not developed enough, such tampering has been on the increase. The "etatistic liberals" in America and elsewhere should be aware of the danger that the reactionaries can exploit, at least partly and temporarily, the popular dislike of tampering by the state and turn it into a resistance against the Welfare State itself, and against planning. Those who stand for progress and reform in our countries may then easily be caught in a position where they defend such tampering, while the reactionaries can depict themselves as standing for freedom.

But quite apart from all tactical considerations, to debureaucratise the state and liberate the people from petty interferences, exerted by authorities above their heads and outside their immediate control, is a progressive cause—today as in Jefferson's time. It can be accomplished only by perfecting and strengthening the Welfare State. The essence of the argument in this book is, that though planning is continually being necessitated by the rising volume of intervention, the purpose and accomplishment of planning in the Welfare State is, in fact, constantly to simplify, and largely to liquidate, old and new intervention: to substitute a few, mostly overall state policies for a growing mesh of detailed and direct ones, and, in particular, to recondition the national community in such a way that for the most part it can be left to the cooperation and collective bargaining of the people themselves, in all sorts of communities and organisations beneath the formal state level, to settle the norms for their living together.

JUAN JOSE AREVALO
BIG BUSINESS AND POLITICS

In some countries there have been strong ties between government and the church, in others between government and the armed forces, the landowners or other powerful groups. In the United States there is a tradition of close and openly accepted ties between government

and business. "The government is just a business," said Harding's
multi-millionaire Secretary of the Treasury Andrew Mellon, "and can
and should be run on business principles." But, many have observed,
American government has not only been favorable to business princi-
ples but to business interests. Although one can cite many instances
to refute the claim that the American government is merely a servant
of Big Business, there still remain the close relations between the
administration and business interests.

Juan José Arévalo was President of Guatemala from 1945 to 1951.
The following pages are taken from chapters 17 and 18 of his bitter
attack on the United States, The Shark and the Sardines *translated*
by June Cobb and Raul Osegueda (New York: Lyle Stuart, 1961),
pp. 233-239, 243-244. Reprinted by permission of the publisher. The
title refers to his fable satirizing the relations between the United
States and the Latin American countries. He had himself experienced
the United States in the role of shark: in 1954 he was forced into
exile when his successor in the Presidency was driven from office by
a coup supported by the United States.

While in the little Central and South American *republiquettes,* the
State continues to be a juridic power; in the United States, the State
as a juridic power has disappeared, caught up slowly and implacably
in the claws of the industrialists and the millionaires. *"L'état c'est*
moi," shouts Wall Street. *"L'état c'est moi,"* shouts the Pentagon.
"I am the Pentagon," corrects General Motors.

Those few representatives and senators and those few court judges
are the ones who uphold the privilege of being independent in the
face of the millionaires' syndicate. These few good men are the last
remains of a juridic state of law that was the greatest stronghold of
democracy at the beginning of the 19th century. They are the rickets-
ridden heirs of one of the world's great men, named Lincoln.

They are the idealists of the old school. They do survive, but they
are backed into a corner, as a ridiculous minority. (From idealism
to pragmatism, and from pragmatism to mercantilism: a 180-degree
turn.)

Unfortunately, such men do not carry a majority on any occasion.
The overwhelming and vociferous majority is nowadays made up of
senators and representatives who are lackeys of monopolies and judges

who "interpret" the laws in an attitude of protection and paternalism. Protection and paternalism of the powerful.

We have just seen how the states of Illinois, Ohio, Massachusetts, Georgia, South Dakota, Montana, Delaware, and New York have an electorate manipulated by forces dependent on the big houses of the millionaires. More profound research would show that more or less the same thing occurs in forty states of the Union. In each one of these states, political advertising is paid for with money from one of the luminaries that we have just mentioned, when not from the National Association of Manufacturers.

And they are so shrewd and so practical that the most antagonistic parties and groups all receive money from the same sources. Whoever wins, the payment-maker is protected.

The Democratic Party is no more independent with respect to Wall Street than the Republican Party—with its dinosaur division. Both have their home base in Wall Street.

So, any candidate who is elected will have a great deal for which to thank the golden oligarchy—and, for that very reason, much to keep quiet about, and much to obey. It is superfluous to point out the danger that the millionaires might get wise and become candidates themselves, taking advantage of the "authority" that comes from the apportioning of electoral funds. In 1949—for just one example—Mr. G. Mennen Williams was chosen Governor of Michigan. He was on the ticket of the Democratic Party, but he was a millionaire who had prospered by manufacturing the Williams Shaving Cream and mentholated Mennen cream, to be used after shaving.

Since then, Nelson Rockefeller has been elected Governor of New York.

Let us not be surprised that the Congress of the United States should, in the long run, turn out to be a conglomerate of captains of business or gentlemen of industry, improvised statesmen, men with hair on their chests, regional bosses, repentant politicians—all of them as disciplined, as constructive, and as collaborationist as the members of the Congress that in 1961 existed in the Dominican Republic under the regime of the multi-millionaire Trujillo (who, at the time of his assassination was said to have stolen sixty percent of the total wealth of his country) or like those that can exist in Nicaragua, under that country's principal businessman, Somoza, who happens to be President of the Republic.

By different routes, democracy, the free world, our glorious West, have arrived at the same situations. And we have taken time for these references to the Congress of the Union because it is there that there are still functionaries pure enough for governmental functions to be attributed to them and pure enough to exercise functions of government, with independent spirit; although they are a tiny minority.

But, as regards government *autonomasia*—that is to say, Executive Power—what we have heard is alarming. We would like very much to have all the facts, to be able to exhibit them. We will content ourselves with recalling the information that reached this extreme South in reliable publications.

First of all, let us mention the phrase that crops up in the United States during election campaigns—"to buy the President." It seems that the presidential candidacy is one of just so many businesses on the New York Stock Exchange. People better informed than I (those privileged to eat hot-dogs within the United States) will be able to furnish documents to round out this list of presidents "elected" by radar, from Wall Street.

As far as I am concerned, it is hard for me to believe that a man of the military glories and the natural *bon-hommerie* of Eisenhower should have been negotiated or bought by Wall Street and the Republican Party. But this does not authorize us to forget that his successor John Kennedy is the son of the number one landlord in the United States or that Calvin Coolidge was President thanks to the ringing and ready money of the House of Morgan, in which Coolidge was a powerful stockholder.

We also know that Herbert Hoover was President, thanks to du Pont de Nemours, a firm to which Hoover had rendered service as confidential informer during the disarmament discussions in 1925, when he was Secretary of Commerce.

The Assistant Secretary of Commerce during the Hoover administration was a gentleman destined to extensive and long enduring enterprises outside the United States. His name was Julius Klein.

We know, and we are obliged to say so, that Senator Henry Cabot Lodge (of the Boston group and lawyer of the House of Morgan) was designated to help direct the electoral campaign that carried General Eisenhower to the Presidency.

Take note that we are speaking here of normal relations (normal in the United States) between the millionaire businessmen and the political leadership of the powerful nation. We do not want to refer to (nor do we have enough documentation to discuss) how ill-gained capital, the capital of criminals, is related to candidates for office as President, Senator, Representative or Governor. There was scandal enough in the world when Senator Thomas J. Walsh denounced the intimate ties between the United States Attorney General, Harry M. Daugherty, and the "Ohio gang"—relations which, when verified and about to be circulated, brought about President Harding's suicide or his assassination by one of his intimates.

But let us set aside the ties between politics and crime. Let us return to the normal relations between business and the statesmen. And let us accept for our escort Harry S. Truman (involuntarily he collaborates with us).

In August of 1955, famous Citizen Truman said:

The Eisenhower administration is dominated by and controlled by big business, which it allows to plunder our natural resources.

Ex-President Truman makes one mistake. He assumes that there are no *compulsory* ties between Wall Street and the government. How soon he forgot the MacArthur case!

By examining the cabinet of the very President (Eisenhower) who was at that moment governing the United States of America, we establish Mr. Truman's error.

Charles E. Wilson, President of General Motors (House of du Pont de Nemours). Wilson was the Secretary of Defense.

Herbert Brownell, Jr., of the Rockefeller Corporation. Brownell was Attorney General.

John J. McCloy, brother-in-law of a director of the House of Morgan and head of Chase Manhattan Bank (Rockefeller). McCloy was Assistant Secretary of War in World War II, President of the World Bank 1947-49, and U. S. Military Governor and High Commissioner of Germany 1949-1952. (In his latter post he pardoned hun-

dreds of Nazi war criminals, extending himself particularly to free-
ing imprisoned industrialist criminals such as Alfred Krupp.)
George Humphrey, magnate in the steel and coal empire. Humphrey
is Secretary of the Treasury.
Sinclair Weeks, multimillionaire of the Boston group. Weeks is
Secretary of Commerce.
Arthur Summerfield, leading Chevrolet dealer and director of the
National Automobile Dealers Association. Summerfield was Post-
master General.

And, finally, the man so well beloved to us, John Foster Dulles,
leader of world destiny since 1953. Dulles, who acted as Secretary
of State, was no less than:

Lawyer of the Wall Street law firm, Sullivan and Cromwell.
Chairman of the Rockefeller Foundation.
Adviser of Standard Oil.
Lawyer of the International Railroads of Central America (in
Guatemala and El Salvador) cell of the United Fruit Company.
Director of American Bank Note Company.
Director of the International Nickel Company.
Director of the Bank of New York.
Counsel Extraordinary in North America (excepting Mexico and
Canada) of Nazi interests in general and Hitlerian interests in par-
ticular.

As can be seen, General Eisenhower did not appear with a Cabinet
made up of men covered with military honors. Only a rogue could
say that Eisenhower was a puppet of the Army!
Let us continue reminiscing:
At the end of the Second World War, the Secretary of State was
Edward R. Stettinius, Director of U. S. Steel.
Another Secretary of State was Dean Acheson, of the firm of
Covington, Burling, Rublee, Acheson and Shorb, and banker of the
associated bankers, Rockefeller, Tweed, Hope, Macley and McCloy.
The Special Assistant to the President in 1951 (and earlier, Secre-
tary of Commerce) was Averell Harriman, banker of the firm Brown
Brothers, Harriman and Company.

Assistant Secretary of State and very famous in our countries was Mr. Spruille Braden of Braden Copper Company.

Under Secretary of State in Charge of Economic Affairs was Mr. William Clayton, cotton magnate, the same one who, at the Chapultepec Conference, proposed the definitive colonization of Latin America.

Another Under Secretary was Mr. Robert E. Olds, who belonged to the House of Morgan and who planted a fake story with the Associated Press aimed to stir up war with Mexico, in aid of the U. S. oil interests.

When Mexico asked for a credit of four hundred million dollars for refining and drilling equipment, it was made known to them that they would receive the credit if they would change their petroleum laws to permit the participation of United States capital. Since the Mexican government resisted the blackmail, the National Petroleum Council of the United States opposed the credit.

But the State Department's close ties to Wall Street are even better demonstrated in the case of Chile and her petroleum. With the naïveté common to sardines, the Chilean nation, wanting to exploit—for Chile!—the deposits in their extreme South (Spring-Hill) applied to the Eximbank for a loan that would allow them to finance the formidable undertaking. In May, 1946, the Yankee bank rejected the application on the grounds that law prohibits the bank from financing projects which private enterprises are willing to undertake.

We should correct the wording of the reply and clarify it in the following terms: *As long as any private Yankee company wants to engage in the economic exploitation of Latin America, no assistance with loans will be given to any competitor, even if a Latin-American nation itself be the one trying to carry out a project.*

In a choice between what would benefit the Chilean nation and what would be of advantage to the plans of the Rockefeller family, the Yankee government have no reason to vacillate in their decision. . . .

Doesn't this give one a chill?

Where does Wall Street begin and where does it end?

Where does the Yankee government begin and where does it end? Does the government still have any juridic significance? Has the juridic given way to utterly mercantile ends and ideals?

Will Wall Street finally bring the State Department into total submission or will the State Department crush the snakes?

A high functionary of the State Department, Mr. James W. Gerard, who was United States Ambassador in Germany, interrupts us, not to rule out the questions, but rather to help us with the answer. In 1930, this ex-Ambassador published a list of the sixty-four men who governed the United States. The list excluded the President of the nation, Mr. Herbert Hoover, because, according to Gerard, Hoover did not take part in the concrete acts of the Government. And among the sixty-four "leaders" of the weightiest democracy of the present day, only one politician was mentioned.

The others were all—all—multimillionaires of banking, industry, and trade. Included, of course, were:

Rockefeller, Mellon, Ford, du Pont de Nemours, Ryan, Morgan, McCormick, Davis, Lamont, Guggenheim, Hearst, Patterson—to mention only those best known in Central and South America. And as rulers of the country, there were on the list: Standard Oil, International Telephone and Telegraph, General Electric, U. S. Steel, Bethlehem Steel, American Tobacco, Electric Bond and Share . . .

I can well imagine the dismay that will fill the hearts of the inhabitants of countries that produce copper, petroleum, iron, meat, lumber, rubber, coffee or tin. Not to be able to turn to the Government of the United States to complain against the voraciousness of the vultures of Wall Street! To realize that the Government is just as voracious!

DANIEL COSIO VILLEGAS
INTELLECTUALS VS. BUSINESSMEN

In his contribution to As Others See Us *(p. 37), Daniel Cosío Villegas, a prominent Mexican economist and civil servant, touched upon another aspect of the issue discussed by Arevalo, the status of the businessman in American society. While the actual power of the influential man of business may not be greater in the United States than in many other countries, Villegas' claim that he is more honored and looked up to deserves further consideration. The following selection is from Daniel Cosío Villegas, "From Mexico," in Franz M. Joseph, As Others See Us: The United States Through Foreign Eyes, pp. 293-296. Reprinted by permission of Princeton University Press.*

The role of the intellectual in North American society is still more revealing of the fact that intelligence and culture have not penetrated very deeply into that society during the last thirty or forty years. The intellectual—the scientist, the writer, or the artist—is not, or has rarely been, an object of general public admiration in the United States. It is true, of course, that he usually enjoys a more comfortable and stable life than his equal anywhere else in the world. We Latin Americans are perhaps more aware of this than anyone else, because in our countries it has not yet occurred that a writer, for example, has been able to make a fortune with his pen. But the same thing can be said of the intellectual in the United States as of the worker or the bureaucrat: he lives better not as a result of any special dispensation, but for the simple reason that he happened to be born in a richer society, and it is inevitable that some of the national abundance should fall to his lot. The point, then, is not his income, but the general esteem accorded him—whether he is an object of admiration, whether he participates in public life, whether he has some influence in it by virtue of being an intellectual, and whether he is a hero or archetype that children and young persons propose to follow or imitate.

Of course it has been many, many years since an intellectual was chief of state. Moreover, when a Presidential candidate like Adlai Stevenson appears (who is not, strictly speaking, an intellectual), then North American society reacts by inventing the derogatory expression "egghead" to express its surprise and scorn at the arrogance of an intellectual who would try to govern it. Not only has there not for a long time been a chief of state or Cabinet member who was an intellectual, but when one has appeared in the Senate or the House of Representatives he has been the exception that proved the rule, the comet that appears every ten or fifteen years. The same can be said, and perhaps with even greater justification, of the local political scene, that of the state, cities, or small towns.

In the United States the elder statesman is Bernard Baruch, a successful businessman, not a Winston Churchill, able to occupy his leisure writing, in a remarkable style, the history of the World War or that of the English-speaking peoples; or an Alexis Léger who, after serving in the Quai d'Orsay for many years, changed his name to write exquisite poetry. Not for a long time, perhaps not since the days of Jefferson, has any public figure in the United States been an object of the public veneration enjoyed by Martí in Cuba or Sarmiento and Mitre in Argentina, to mention three intellectuals who served their countries. Since the time of Franklin has there been a Paul Claudel in American diplomacy, to say nothing of a Goethe? What writer has ever occupied the place that was at one time occupied on the stage of all French life by Victor Hugo? Among the interpreters of American life has there been even one François Mauriac, Chesterton, or Ortega y Gasset? Did not Albert Einstein turn out to be a little disturbing for the United States—not, to be sure, as a physicist, but as a human being? And ultimately did not Charlie Chaplin prove too disconcerting?

It is undeniable that the archetype of North American society, the model or the hero to be imitated, is not the scholar or even the intelligent man, but the successful businessman—the man of humble origin, largely unlettered, who succeeds, through his tenacity and cleverness, in amassing a fabulous fortune. He is the ideal because his story is what actually happens in American life, and also because it occurs with much greater frequency than any other example of social success. Moreover, all education that the child receives, from his parents or in the school, is conducive to building that model. The youth spends his vacation not in rest or in intellectual self-improvement, but in earning money, selling magazines, or washing dishes and glasses in a soda fountain. I have been told that in Japan, at least in the period between the two world wars, the great lesson of life that the father wished to teach his son was that a man cannot, and should not, put his trust in any other human being, even his father. In old Spain the great moral lesson that the father spared no pains to inculcate in his children was that of loyalty, that is, fidelity to a given pledge, even though the consequences of keeping it might prove disastrous. Well, the great moral lesson that the North American father respects and teaches his children is the need for self-sufficiency, and to this end they should work, earn money, and know how to handle it wisely—in other words, handle money to earn more money.

The idealization of the businessman—like its opposite, the uncon-cern for the intellectual—has effects in North American political life. Of all the countries in the world the United States is the only one that has not been able to create a group of people who make public service their lifetime concern and are capable, through training and experience, of assuming major responsibility in administration and foreign affairs. In the United States it rarely happens that such dedicated "public servants" reach positions of administrative power. The rule is that administrative matters are handled at the lower levels by an inert bureaucracy, and in the upper echelons by the businessman or the professional who has lived, and will again live, for private instead of public interests.

What is important here is not simply the facts but the philosophy that underlies them. I understand that among the qualifications advanced at the time to justify the appointment of John Foster Dulles as Secretary of State was the fact that for many years he had been associated with a law firm representing the interests of large interna-tional business combines. And I recall very well that at a more recent date the Department of State published a *curriculum vitae* of Mr. Henry Holland—who had just been designated Assistant Secretary for Latin American affairs—of which the outstanding feature was the fact that Mr. Holland belonged to a law firm having interests in Mexico.

Now then, why can this and so many other similar facts have par-ticular significance? Because in as modest a country as Mexico, not only would it be considered an inexcusable lack of tact to name as ambassador to Washington a great coffee exporter or an importer of North American machinery, but the candidate's having such interests would make the appointment absolutely impossible. Undoubtedly it is believed in the United States that having defended the commercial interests of large international combines gave Mr. John Foster Dulles the invaluable experience of discovering that the world is round, varied, and complex; and that Mr. Holland's receipt of financial benefit from Mexico predisposed him, presumably from gratitude, to love Mexico.

It is unquestionable that basically all of this arises from the Ameri-can idea that the only road, or at least the most positive road, to knowledge and experience is the road of business, and not, for exam-ple, the less exposed one of books. Such a notion is not only wrong;

it is harmful to the United States, because experience has shown over and over again that outside the United States it is considered axiomatic that a man closely identified with certain material interests will continue to look out for them, not only when he is in charge of them as businessman or lawyer, but also if he is temporarily in government.

V. AMERICAN WAYS OF LIFE

The folkways of American society are of course too varied to allow sweeping generalizations: there would seem to be few points of resemblance between the mores of the big city slum and the mid-western farm. Nevertheless, some traits or characteristics will all over the world be thought of as typically American, just as we have certain images of what is typically German, English or Japanese. Americans who go abroad—tourists, soldiers or businessmen—are in no small degree responsible for the popular images of the typical American.

The American way of life has long been an established concept (either for abuse or praise) and one dominant theme in the writings of foreigners on America is the more or less vague fear of "Americanization" of their own culture. The following selections present some of the many observations on Americans at home and at work, at school and at play.

What social functions does religion play in America? Do Americans equate morality with religion? Do they equate morality with business morality? With sexual morality? Has there been a change in the last seventy years? In what ways are American eating habits conditioned by their economic system? How do the public schools "Americanize" the country's young people? What does it mean to "Americanize" an immigrant child? Does this education make for diversity or regimentation? In what ways are sports the best "Americanizers" of all? In what ways does "dating" foster regimentation in American society? Why is "love"—or the illusion of love—a typically American emphasis in personal relationships? Does America have *a* sexual morality? How does television reduce American individuality?

MAX WEBER
THE PROTESTANT SECTS AND THE SPIRIT OF CAPITALISM

The following excerpts are taken from an article written by Max Weber in 1906 as a companion piece to his seminal work, The Protestant Ethic and the Spirit of Capitalism *(1904-05; English translation, 1930). This is not the place to summarize Weber's argument showing that the rise of capitalism was closely related to the rise of Protestantism, but it is relevant to note that when he tried to define "the spirit of capitalism" he turned "to a document of that spirit which contains what we are looking for in almost classical purity": the writings of Benjamin Franklin.*

The text below is from Max Weber: Essays in Sociology, *edited and translated by H. H. Gerth and C. Wright Mills. (London: Routledge & Kegan Paul, 1948), pp. 302-308. Copyright 1946 by Oxford University Press, Inc. Reprinted by permission.*

For some time in the United States a principled 'separation of state and church' has existed. This separation is carried through so strictly that there is not even an official census of denominations, for it would be considered against the law for the state even to ask the citizen for his denomination. We shall not here discuss the practical importance of this principle of the relation between religious organizations and the state. We are interested, rather, in the fact that scarcely two and a half decades ago the number of 'persons with church affiliation' in the U.S.A. was estimated to be only about 6 percent; and this despite the absence of all those highly effective premiums which most of the European states then placed upon affiliation with certain privileged churches and despite the immense immigration to the U.S.A.

It should be realized, in addition, that church affiliation in the U.S.A. brings with it incomparably higher financial burdens, especially for the poor, than anywhere in Germany. Published family budgets prove this, and I have personally known of many burdened cases in a congregation in a city on Lake Erie, which was almost entirely composed of German immigrant lumberjacks. Their regular contributions for religious purposes amounted to almost $80 annually, being paid out of an average annual income of about $1,000. Everyone knows that even a small fraction of this financial burden in Germany would lead to a mass exodus from the church. But quite apart from that, nobody who visited the United States fifteen or twenty years ago, that is, before the recent Europeanization of the country began, could overlook the very intense church-mindedness which then prevailed in all regions not yet flooded by European immigrants. Every old travel book reveals that formerly church-mindedness in America went unquestioned, as compared with recent decades, and was even far stronger. Here we are especially interested in one aspect of this situation.

Hardly a generation ago when businessmen were establishing themselves and making new social contacts, they encountered the question: "To what church do you belong?" This was asked unobtrusively and in a manner that seemed to be apropos, but evidently it was never asked accidentally. Even in Brooklyn, New York's twin city, this older tradition was retained to a strong degree, and the more so in communities less exposed to the influence of immigration.*

If one looked more closely at the matter in the United States, one could easily see that the question of religious affiliation was almost always posed in social life and in business life which depended on permanent and credit relations. However, as mentioned above, the American authorities never posed the question. Why?

First, a few personal observations [from 1904] may serve as illustrations. On a long railroad journey through what was then Indian territory, the author, sitting next to a traveling salesman of 'undertaker's hardware' (iron letters for tombstones), casually mentioned the still impressively strong church-mindedness. Thereupon the salesman remarked, "Sir, for my part everybody may believe or not believe

---

*This question reminds one of the typical Scotch *table d'hote*, where a quarter of a century ago the continental European on Sundays almost always had to face the situation of a lady's asking, 'What service did you attend today?' Or, if the Continental, as the oldest guest, should happen to be seated at the head of the table, the waiter when serving the soup would ask him: 'Sir, the prayer, please.' In Portree (Skye) on one beautiful Sunday I faced this typical question and did not know any better way out than to remark 'I am a member of the *Badische Landeskirche* and could not find a chapel of my church in Portree.' The ladies were pleased and satisfied with the answer. 'Oh, he doesn't attend any service except that of his own denomination!'

as he pleases; but if I saw a farmer or a businessman not belonging to any church at all, I wouldn't trust him with fifty cents. Why pay me, if he doesn't believe in anything?'' Now that was a somewhat vague motivation.

The matter became somewhat clearer from the story of a German-born nose-and-throat specialist, who had established himself in a large city on the Ohio River and who told me of the visit of his first patient. Upon the doctor's request, he lay down upon the couch to be examined with the [aid of a] nose reflector. The patient sat up once and remarked with dignity and emphasis, 'Sir, I am a member of the —— Baptist Church in —— Street.' Puzzled about what meaning this circumstance might have for the disease of the nose and its treatment, the doctor discreetly inquired about the matter from an American colleague. The colleague smilingly informed him that the patient's statement of his church membership was merely to say: 'Don't worry about the fees.' But *why* should it mean precisely that? Perhaps this will become still clearer from a third happening.

On a beautiful clear Sunday afternoon early in October I attended a baptism ceremony of a Baptist congregation. I was in the company of some relatives who were farmers in the backwoods some miles out of M. [a county seat] in North Carolina. The baptism was to take place in a pool fed by a brook which descended from the Blue Ridge Mountains, visible in the distance. It was cold and it had been freezing during the night. Masses of farmers' families were standing all around the slopes of the hills; they had come, some from great distances, some from the neighborhood, in their light two-wheeled buggies.

The preacher in a black suit stood waist deep in the pond. After preparations of various sorts, about ten persons of both sexes in their Sunday-best stepped into the pond, one after another. They avowed their faith and then were immersed completely—the women in the preacher's arms. They came up, shaking and shivering in their wet clothes, stepped out of the pond, and everybody 'congratulated' them. They were quickly wrapped in thick blankets and then they drove home. One of my relatives commented that 'faith' provides unfailing protection against sneezes. Another relative stood beside me and, being unchurchly in accordance with German traditions, he looked on, spitting disdainfully over his shoulder. He spoke to one of those baptised, 'Hello, Bill, wasn't the water pretty cool?' and received the very earnest reply, 'Jeff, I thought of some pretty hot place (Hell!), and so I didn't mind the cool water.' During the immersion of one of the young men, my relative was startled.

'Look at him,' he said. 'I told you so!'

When I asked him after the ceremony, 'Why did you anticipate the baptism of that man?' he answered, 'Because he wants to open a bank in M.'

'Are there so many Baptists around that he can make a living?'

'Not at all, but once being baptised he will get the patronage of the whole region and he will outcompete everybody.'

Further questions of 'why' and 'by what means' led to the following conclusion: Admission to the local Baptist congregation follows only upon the most careful 'probation' and after closest inquiries into conduct going back to early childhood (Disorderly conduct? Frequenting taverns? Dance? Theatre? Card Playing? Untimely meeting of liability? Other Frivolities?) The congregation still adhered strictly to the religious tradition.

Admission to the congregation is recognized as an absolute guarantee of the moral qualities of a gentleman, especially of those qualities required in business matters. Baptism secures to the individual the deposits of the whole region and unlimited credit without any competition. He is a 'made man.' Further observation confirmed that these, or at least very similar phenomena, recur in the most varied regions. In general, *only* those men had success in business who belonged to Methodist or Baptist or other *sects* or sectlike conventicles. When a sect member moved to a different place, or if he was a traveling salesman, he carried the certificate of his congregation with him; and thereby he found not only easy contact with sect members but, above all, he found credit everywhere. If he got into economic straits through no fault of his own, the sect arranged his affairs, gave guarantees to the creditors, and helped him in every way, often according to the Biblical principle, *mutuum date nihil inde sperantes*. (Luke vi:35)

The expectation of the creditors that his sect, for the sake of their prestige, would not allow creditors to suffer losses on behalf of a sect member was not, however, decisive for his opportunities. What was decisive was the fact that a fairly reputable sect would only accept for membership one whose 'conduct' made him appear to be morally *qualified* beyond doubt.

It is crucial that sect membership meant a certificate of moral qualification and especially of business morals for the individual. This stands in contrast to membership in a 'church' into which one is 'born' and which lets grace shine over the righteous and the unrighteous alike. Indeed, a church is a corporation which organizes grace and administers religious gifts of grace, like an endowed foundation. Affiliation with the church is, in principle, obligatory and hence proves nothing with regard to the member's qualities. A sect, however, is a voluntary association of only those who, according to the principle, are religiously and morally qualified. If one finds voluntary reception of his membership, by virtue of religious *probation,* he joins the sect voluntarily.

It is, of course, an established fact that this selection has often been very strongly counteracted, precisely in America, through the proselyting of souls by competing sects, which, in part, was strongly determined by the material interests of the preachers. Hence, cartels for the restriction of proselyting have frequently existed among the competing denominations. Such cartels were formed, for instance, in order to exclude the easy wedding of a person who had been divorced for reasons which, from a religious point of view, were considered insufficient. Religious organizations that facilitated remarriage had great attraction. Some Baptist communities are said at times to have been lax in this respect, whereas the Catholic as well as the Lutheran (Missouri) churches were praised for their strict correctness. This correctness, however, allegedly reduced the membership of both churches.

Expulsion from one's sect for moral offenses has meant, economically, loss of credit and, socially, being declassed.

Numerous observations during the following months confirmed not only that church-mindedness *per se,* although still (1904) rather important, was rapidly dying out; but the particularly important trait, mentioned above, was definitely confirmed. In metropolitan areas I was spontaneously told, in several cases, that a speculator in undeveloped real estate would regularly erect a church building, often an extremely modest one; then he would hire a candidate from one of the various theological seminaries, pay him $500 to $600, and hold out to him a splendid position as a preacher for life if he would gather a congregation and thus preach the building terrain 'full. Deteriorated churchlike structures which marked failures were shown to me. For the most part, however, the preachers were said to be successful. Neighborly contact, Sunday School, and so on, were said to be indispensable to the newcomer, but above all association with 'morally' reliable neighbors.

Competition among sects is strong, among other things, through the kind of material and spiritual offerings at evening teas of the congregations. Among genteel churches also, musical presentations contribute to this competition. (A tenor in Trinity Church, Boston, who allegedly had to sing on Sundays *only*, at that time received $8,000.) Despite this sharp competition, the sects often maintained fairly good mutual relations. For instance, in the service of the Methodist church which I attended, the Baptist ceremony of the baptism, which I mentioned above, was recommended as a spectacle to edify everybody. In the main, the congregations refused entirely to listen to the preaching of 'dogma' and to confessional distinctions. 'Ethics' alone could be offered. In those instances where I listened to sermons for the middle classes, the typical bourgeois morality, respectable and solid, to be sure, and of the most homely and sober kind, was preached. But the sermons were delivered with obvious inner conviction; the preacher was often moved.

Today the kind of denomination [to which one belongs] is rather irrelevant. It does not matter whether one be Freemason, Christian Scientist, Adventist, Quaker, or what not. What is decisive is that one be admitted to membership by 'ballot,' after an *examination* and an ethical *probation* in the sense of the virtues which are at a premium for the inner-worldly asceticism of protestantism and hence, for the ancient puritan tradition. Then, the same effect could be observed.

Closer scrutiny revealed the steady progress of the characteristic process of 'secularization,' to which in modern times all phenomena that originated in religious conceptions succumb. Not only religious associations, hence sects, had this effect on American life. Sects exercised this influence, rather, in a steadily decreasing proportion. If one paid some attention it was striking to observe (even fifteen years ago) that surprisingly many men among the American middle classes (always outside of the quite modern metropolitan areas and the immigra-

tion centers) were wearing a little badge (of varying color) in the but-
tonhole, which reminded one very closely of the rosette of the French
Legion of Honor.

When asked what it meant, people regularly mentioned an association with a sometimes adventurous and fantastic name. And it became
obvious that its significance and purpose consisted in the following:
Almost always the association functioned as a burial insurance,
besides offering greatly varied services. But often, and especially in
those areas least touched by modern disintegration, the association
offered the member the (ethical) claim for brotherly help on the part
of every brother who had the means. If he faced an economic emer-
gency for which he himself was not to be blamed, he could make
this claim. And in several instances that came to my notice at the
time, this claim again followed the very principle, *mutuum date nihil
inde sperantes,* or at least a very low rate of interest prevailed. Apparently, such claims were willingly recognized by the members of the
brotherhood. Furthermore—and this is the main point in this instance
—membership was again acquired through balloting after investigation
and a determination of moral worth. And hence the badge in the but-
tonhole meant, 'I am a gentleman patented after investigation and
probation and guaranteed by my membership.' Again, this meant, in
business life above all, tested *credit worthiness*. One could observe
that business opportunities were often decisively influenced by such
legitimation.

All these phenomena, which seemed to be rather rapidly disintegrat-
ing—at least the religious organizations—were essentially confined to
the middle classes. Some cultured Americans often dismissed these
facts briefly and with a certain angry disdain as 'humbug' or
backwardness, or they even denied them; many of them actually did
not know anything about them, as was affirmed to me by William
James. Yet these survivals were still alive in many different fields,
and sometimes in forms which appeared to be grotesque.

These associations were especially the typical vehicles of social
ascent into the circle of the entrepreneurial middle class. They served
to diffuse and to maintain the bourgeois capitalist business ethos
among the broad strata of the middle classes (the farmers included).

GEORGES DUHAMEL
SEX AND THE LAW

Georges Duhamel's America the Menace: Scenes from the Life of the Future *(1931) reveals more of the French author's prejudices than a view of American society. He hated the cinema ("a most powerful instrument for enforcing a uniform standard, alike in ethics, politics, and aesthetics"), recorded music ("It was imitation music, canned music. It came from the slaughter-house of music, as the breakfast sausages came from the slaughter-house of swine.") and the automobile ("that increases all our vices, and that does not exalt our virtues"). But to his critics, who may not recognize their America in his violent diatribe, he retorts: "America? I am not talking of America. By means of this America I am questioning the future; I am trying to determine the path that, willy-nilly, we must follow."*

The following passages are taken from the translation by Charles Miner Thompson (London: George Allen & Unwin, 1931), pp. 175-179. Copyright 1931 by Houghton Mifflin Company. Copyright © renewed 1959 by Houghton Mifflin Company. Reprinted by permission of Houghton Mifflin Company.

At the Pennsylvania Station a porter, majestic as a Cathedral verger, glanced an order at one of his minions to take my baggage.

I was not lost, I was not abandoned in this grim, bustling crowd that was noisy and taciturn at the same time. That sisterly, watchful glance, that glance which is so vivacious, so frank, I must say so French, and especially so easy to interpret, is that of—what shall I christen her for my friendly archives?—is that of, let us say Mademoiselle Greatheart.

'I am going to go up to your room,' she said, 'and see whether you're comfortably settled. I will give you your letters, and show you the ropes.'

We started. How the elevator flew! Following the bell-boy, we began our search for the room that was hidden so thoroughly in this labyrinthine building.

At last! The bell-boy lighted the lamps, put down the bags, and stood at attention. On his lips was a smile that I knew well, for I have often seen it blossom in this home of the tip. I understood. I took a quarter from my purse. The boy pocketed it, muttered an indifferent 'thank you,' smiled again, and did not budge. In three words, I gave him to understand that I was obliged for his services, but that he was free to depart. Then, bringing his heels together, laying his little finger along the seam of his trouser leg and fixing his gaze on space, the boy came to attention, and in an authoritative voice, that voice as of a loud-speaker that you imagine the voice of the Law to be, recited: 'The gentleman will please ask the lady to leave the chamber at once. Until the lady has left, the gentleman must leave the door open.'

Thereupon, he saluted, about-faced, and without closing the door, gained the hallway, where I heard him walking to and fro.

A gust of anger rose, swelled, and choked me. I had a keen desire to break something, a strong impulse to shout out at the top of my voice the word that in France expresses anger, despair, rebellion, and the resolution to die rather than surrender.

But Greatheart smiled. She had lived for a long time among these dragons of virtue. The vulgarity of the laws no longer made her blush. She obeyed and left. 'I will wait for you,' she said, 'in the hall on this story. There two friends may freely discuss their affairs.'

The same place, the next evening. I was leaving the bathroom, that fabulous bathroom which the economists and the sociologists vie in praising. It is the noblest victory of American pride.

It was warm. The radiator was having its last fit of the evening. I crossed the bedroom to get my pyjamas. Solitude, solitude!

Then suddenly the door, which by chance I had forgotten to lock, came open. A lady appeared in it—shingle, short skirt, rouge, powder, pearls, and diamonds.

She contemplated with interest the person thus surprised in his privacy, and observed, with the completest calm, 'My mistake. Beg pardon.'

Would I not be thoroughly justified, I thought, in dragging that lady into court and demanding heavy damages? Oh, if I only had had witnesses! Oh, if only the bell-boy had been there, that vigilant guardian angel of my blushes!

The same place, five days later. Greatheart knocked at my door.

She was laden with letters—news from home, sad news, for some one whom I loved was dead.

I was far from my native country, from my home, from my love. With my chin upon my breast, I gave myself up to bitter reflection. One who was part of my life was no longer anything but a memory. In my heart of hearts I found the world sad. Greatheart looked at me, and her eyes filled with tears.

Then suddenly the telephone rang piercingly. 'Hurry, Monsieur,' it said, 'hurry; grasp the receiver, and listen, listen!'

At once I recognized that puppet voice. Again the law spoke. 'We know,' it said, 'that a lady has entered your room. Be good enough to open the door and ask this woman, who is not provided with the special authorization, to leave at once.'

'Very well, my friend,' said I to Greatheart, 'let us go. I am not today in any condition to resist. I have not the least desire to laugh, but . . .'

ILYA ILF AND EUGENE PETROV
APPETITE DEPARTS WHILE EATING

The subtitle of Ilya Ilf and Eugene Petrov's Little Golden America *is "Two Famous Soviet Humorists Survey the United States." The fame of these two writers rested on their* Little Golden Calf *(1932), a humorous account of life in the Soviet Union. In 1935 they were commissioned to write an account of the United States. The result was an entertaining and often surprisingly friendly narrative of their journey from coast to coast. From the very beginning they were disenchanted with American cooking, which reached the lowest level at the drug-store counter: "We looked sadly at the menu. Dinner # 1, Dinner # 2, Dinner # 3, Dinner # 4—Dinner Number One, Dinner Number Two, Dinner Number Three, Dinner Number Four! Dinner # 4 costs twice as much as Dinner # 2, but that doesn't mean that it is twice as good. No! There is simply twice as much of it. If in Dinner # 2 a course called country sausage consists of three chopped off sausages, then in Dinner # 4 there will be six chopped off sausages, but the taste will be exactly the same."*

We left the hotel to lunch somewhere, and soon found ourselves on Forty-second Street. During our first days in New York, no matter where we were bound for, we invariably landed on Forty-second Street.

In the crowd, which carried us along, we heard shreds of that quick New York speech which surely must be as strange to the ear of a Londoner as it is to the ear of a Muscovite. Along the walls sat boys—bootblacks, who drummed their brushes on their crudely fashioned wooden boxes, touting for customers. Street photographers aimed their cameras at the passers-by, choosing usually ladies with escorts or tourists from the sticks. After clicking his camera, the photographer would approach the object of his attack and press on him the printed address of his studio. For twenty-five cents the photographed pedestrian may have a candid photograph of himself, a splendid photograph, in the uninhibited act of raising his leg.

Under the sooty spans of a bridge, in the shadow of which gleamed mud left over from last night's rain, a man with hat aslant and an open shirt was delivering a speech. About a score of the curious gathered around him. He was a propagandist for the ideas of the recently assassinated United States senator from Louisiana, Huey P. Long. He spoke on distribution of wealth. His listeners asked him questions. He replied. His chief task seemed to be to amuse his audience. Not far from him, on the sunflecked sidewalk, stopped a fat Negress of the Salvation Army. She wore an old-fashioned bonnet and run-down shoes. She took a bell out of her suitcase and rang it loudly. The suitcase she placed on the sidewalk at her feet. After waiting for a few disciples of the late-lamented senator to desert to her side, squinting against the sun, she began to bellow something, rolling her eyes and banging her own fat bosom. We went several blocks, but the shouting of the Negress was still distinctly heard in the component noise of this restless city.

In front of a ready-to-wear store a man walked calmly back and forth. On his back and on his chest he carried two identical placards: 'This Place Is On Strike.'' In the next street were a few more pickets. Over the large show window of a corner store, despite the sunny morning, gleamed the blue letters "Cafeteria" in electric lights. The cafeteria was large, bright, and clean. Along the walls were glass cases filled with beautiful, appetizing edibles. To the left of the entrance was the cashier's booth. On the right was a metal stand with small slot athwart as in a coin bank. From the opening emerged the end of a blue pasteboard stub. Those who entered tugged at this end. We also tugged. The melodic clang of a bell resounded. One stub was in our hand, and through the slot of the coin bank another blue stub popped out. Then we did what all New Yorkers do when they dash into a cafeteria for a hurried bite. From a special table we each took a light brown tray, placed on it forks, spoons, knives, and paper napkins; and, feeling extremely awkward in our heavy overcoats and hats, went to the right end of a glass-enclosed counter. Down the entire length of this counter ran three rows of nickelled pipes on which we conveniently placed our trays and slid them along after placing each dish upon them. The counter itself was a tremendous camouflaged electric plate. Soups, chunks of roast, sausages of various lengths and thicknesses, legs of pork and lamb, meat loaves and roulades, mashed, fried, baked, and boiled potatoes and potatoes curiously shaped in pellets, globules of Brussels sprouts, spinach, carrots, and numerous other side dishes were kept warm here. White chefs in starched nightcaps, aided by neat but heavily rouged and marcelled girls in pink headdresses, were busy placing on the glass cover of the counter plates of food and punching that figure on the stub which indicated the cost of each dish. Then came salads and vinaigrettes, various hors d'oeuvres, fish in cream sauces and fish in jellied sauces. Then came bread, rolls, and traditional round pies with apple, strawberry, and pineapple fillings. Here coffee and milk were issued. We moved down the counter, pushing our trays. On the thick layer of chipped ice were plates of compotes and ice-cream, oranges and grapefruit cut in half, large and small glasses with various juices. Persistent advertising has taught Americans to drink juices before breakfast and lunch. In the juices are vitamins which are presumably beneficial to the customers, while the sale of juices is indubitably of benefit to fruit merchants. We soon succumbed to this American custom. At first we drank the thick yellow orange juice. Then we passed to the translucent green juice of the grapefruit. Then before eating we began to take the grapefruit itself (it is covered with sugar and is eaten with a spoon; its taste reminds one somewhat of the taste of an orange with a dash of lemon in it, although it is juicier than both these fruits). Finally, with some trepidation and not all at once, we began to imbibe the mundane tomato juice, peppering it a bit beforehand. That proved to be the tastiest of all and the most refreshing, and it best suited our South Russian stomachs. The one thing we did not learn to do in America was to eat melon before dinner. Yet that takes the place of honour among American hors d'oeuvres.

In the middle of the cafeteria stood polished wooden tables without tablecloths, and beside them coat-racks. Those who wished could put their hats under their chairs, where there was a special shelf for that purpose. On the tables were stands with bottles of oil, vinegar, catsup, and various other condiments. There was also granulated sugar in a glass flagon wrought in the manner of a pepper-shaker with holes in its metal stopper.

The settling of accounts with the customers was simple. No one could leave the cafeteria without sooner or later passing the cashier's booth and presenting the stub with the total punched in it: Here also cigarettes were sold and one was free to take a toothpick.

The process of eating was just as superbly rationalized as the production of automobiles or of typewriters.

The automats have progressed farther along this road than the cafeterias. Although they have approximately the same outward appearance as the cafeterias, they differ from the latter in that they have carried the process of pushing food into American stomachs to the point of virtuosity. The walls of the automats are occupied throughout with little glass closets. Near each one of them is a slit for dropping a "nickel" (a five-cent coin). Behind the glass stands a dour sandwich or a glass of juice or a piece of pie. Despite the shining glass and metal, the sausages and cutlets deprived of liberty somehow produce a strange impression. One pities them, like cats at a show. A man drops a nickel, acquires the right to open the little door, takes out his sandwich, carries it to his table and there eats it, again putting his hat under his chair on the special shelf. Then the man goes up to a tap, drops his "nickel," and out of the tap into the glass drips exactly as much coffee and milk as is supposed to drip. One feels something humiliating, something insulting to man in that. One begins to suspect that the owner of the automat has outfitted his establishment, not in order to present society with a pleasant surprise, but in order to discharge from service poor marcelled girls with pink headdresses and thereby earn a few more dollars.

But automats are not over popular in America. Evidently the bosses themselves feel that there must be some limit to rationalization. Hence, the normal little restaurants, for people of modest means, belonging to mighty trusts are always full. The most popular of these—Childs—has become in America a standard for inexpensive food of good quality. "He dines at Childs": that means that the man earns $30 a week. In any part of New York one can say: "Let's have dinner at Childs," and it would not take him more than ten minutes to reach Childs. At Childs one receives the same clean handsome food as in a cafeteria or an automat. Only there one is not deprived of the small satisfaction of looking at a menu, saying "H'm," asking the waitress whether the veal is good, and receiving the answer: "Yes, sir!"

Generally speaking, New York is remarkable because it has everything. There you can find the representatives of any nation, secure any dish, any object from an embroidered Ukranian shirt to a Chinese stick with a bone handle in the shape of a hand, which is used for back-scratching, from Russian caviare and vodka to Chilean soup and Italian macaroni. There are no delicacies in the world that New York cannot offer. But for all of it one must pay in dollars. And we want to talk about the preponderant majority of Americans who can pay only cents and for whom exist Childs, cafeterias, and automats. When describing the latter establishments, we can boldly declare that this is how the average American is fed. Under this concept of the average American is presupposed a man who has a decent job and a decent salary and who from the point of view of capitalism is an example of the healthy prospering American, happy and optimistic, who receives all the blessings of life at a comparatively low price.

The splendid organization of the restaurant business seems to confirm that. Model cleanliness, good quality of produce, an extensive choice of dishes, a minimum of time lost in dining. All that is so. But here is the trouble. All this beautifully prepared food is quite tasteless—colourless in taste. It is not injurious to the stomach. It is most likely even of benefit to it. But it does not present man with any delights, any gustatory satisfaction. When you select in the closets of the automat or on the counter of the cafeteria an attractive piece of roast, and then eat it at your table, having shoved your hat under your chair, you feel like a buyer of shoes which proved to be more handsome than substantial. Americans are used to it. They eat fast, without wasting a single extra minute at the table. They do not eat; they fill up on food, just as an automobile is filled with petrol. The French gourmet who can sit four hours at a dinner, chewing each piece of meat in exultation, washing it down with wine and then smacking every mouthful of coffee with cognac—he is, of course, no model man. But the cold American eater, bereft of the natural human desire to get some satisfaction out of food, evokes amazement.

For a long time we could not understand why American dishes, so appetizing in appearance, are so unappealing in taste. At first we thought the Americans simply do not know how to cook. But then we learned that that alone is not the point: the crux of the matter is in the organization itself, in the very essence of the American economic system. Americans eat a blindingly white but utterly tasteless bread, frozen meat, salty butter, unripe tomatoes, and canned goods.

How does it happen that the richest country in the world, a country of grain growers and cattle raisers, of gold and remarkable industry, a country which has sufficient resources to create a paradise, cannot give the people tasty bread, fresh meat, real butter, and ripe tomatoes?

Near New York we saw waste places overgrown with weeds, forsaken plots of earth. No one sowed grain there, no one raised cattle there. We saw there neither setting hens with chicks nor truck gardens.

"You see," we were told, "it simply would not pay. We cannot compete here with the monopolists from the West."

Somewhere in Chicago, in the slaughter-houses, they kill cattle and transport the meat throughout the country in frozen form. From somewhere in California they ship frozen chickens, and green tomatoes which are supposed to ripen in transit. And no one dares to challenge the mighty monopolists to a fight.

Sitting in a cafeteria, we read Mikoyan's speech, which said that food in a socialist country must be palatable—that it must bring joy to people—and it sounded like poetry to us.

While in America the business of feeding people, as any other business is built on this single consideration: does it pay or does it not pay? It does not pay to raise cattle and to have truck gardens in New York. Therefore, people eat frozen meat, salty butter, and unripe tomatoes. Some business man discovers that it pays to sell chewing gum, so people are taught to chew this cud. Cinema pays better than theatre; therefore, cinema develops while the theatre is neglected, although from a cultural standpoint the American theatre is much more important than the cinema. The elevated brings an income to certain companies; therefore New Yorkers become martyrs. Along Broadway, through all the crowded traffic, with a hellish screeching, a street-car hobbles along—only because it pays one man, the owner of an ancient street-car company.

All the time we were there we felt an irresistible desire common to all Soviet people to complain and to offer suggestions. We wanted to write to the Soviet control and to the party control and to the Central Committee and to *Pravda,* but there was no one to complain to, and there is no such thing in America as "a book of suggestions."

DENIS W. BROGAN
LEARNING TO LIVE IN AMERICA

Few have written so much and with such excellence about the United States as the British political scientist Denis W. Brogan. His analysis of the "Americanization" function of the American schools is from The American Character, *a book as valuable today as when it first appeared in 1944. Still, some may wonder what is to take the place of the Americanization rituals as this function gradually becomes less important. Others may counter that some aspects of the Americanization process will remain a central task for the American school system for several generations to come. The following excerpts are taken from pp. 135-143 of the New York edition of the American Character, by Denis W. Brogan. Copyright 1944 by Denis W. Brogan. Reprinted by permission of Alfred A. Knopf, Inc.*

The word "school", in America covers every type of educational institution. Being "at school" may mean being at a kindergarten or at Harvard. School, too, has kept much of its Greek meaning. It is a system of organization and training for leisure as well as work. And t has become more and more adjusted to its environment, undertaking to do more than it can (which is very American) and doing much more than it seems to do (which is also very American).

The social and political role of American education cannot be understood if it is thought of as being primarily a means of formal instruction. If it is so thought of, it will be overrated and underrated. It will be overrated because the figures of two million college students, of seven million high school students, will dazzle the visitor used to seeing opportunities for higher education doled out (except in Soviet Russia) on a combined class-and-intellectual basis. It will be underrated if, at any stage below the highest (that is, below the great universities), the academic standards are compared with those of a good English, French, or pre-Hitler German school. If these millions of boys and girls are to be judged by their academic accomplishments, they will be judged harshly. But they are not to be so judged, for heir schools are doing far more than instruct them: they are letting them instruct each other in how to live in America.

Of those millions, a large section will be the children of immigrants to whom English is still largely a foreign tongue. Of these millions, a very large proportion will be the children of migrants from different parts of the United States. Others will be the children of rural-bred parents, forced to adjust themselves to the new urban world. They have to learn a common language, common habits, common tolerances, a common political and national faith. And they do. It is this aim and this success that justifies the lavish buildings of the local high school; not merely the classrooms and the laboratories, but the gymnasium, the field-house where basketball can be played in comfort in the depth of the bitter winter, the swimming pools in which the summer heat can be endured.

It is true that the teachers are relatively badly paid and have an inferior social as well as economic standing, insecure tenure and politics making their condition worse. More money spent on men might get better results than more money spent on buildings. But it is easier to get the materials for buildings than the materials for teachers. As

long as American society remains individualistic, competitive, confident that the answers to the present are in the future, not in the past,
   is going to take more than money to seduce the right men and women in adequate numbers away from the life of action. And, a point too seldom remembered, the necessity for providing teachers for the two million college students hampers recruiting for high schools. In many cases, the colleges are doing what is really high school work ind it matters comparatively little where the good teachers are, as ong as they are teaching.

   The political function of the schools is to teach Americanism, meaning not merely political and patriotic dogma, but the habits necessary to American life. This justifies the most extravagant items in the curriculum. Since the ability to play bridge is one of the marks of Americanism in a suburb, it is reasonable that there should be bridge clubs in schools. The main political achievement of the high schools and grammar schools is to bring together the young of all classes and all origins, to provide, artificially, the common background that in an old, rural society is provided by tradition, by the necessary collaboration of village life. The elementary schools—the "grade" schools —do this, too, but as far as an American town is broken up into racial blocs, the Ethan Allen Public School may have mainly Polish pupils, the Zachary Chandler mainly Welsh. Only in the Warren G. Harding High School is a big enough common pool formed in which Americans can be made.

   Some of that Americanization is, of course, done deliberately and formally. Mr. Carlton Hayes pointed out long ago that the ritual of flag worship and oath-taking in an American school is a religious observance. Little boys and girls, in a school from which religion in the old sense is barred, solemnly rising each morning and reciting together the "American's Creed" are performing a religious exercise as truly as if they began the day with "I believe in God the Father Almighty" or asserted that "There is no God but God." . . .

   The flag worship of the American school and the American nation was brought home to the British public in an episode that, if funny, was also very revealing. For the London makers of ladies' underwear who adorned their garments with American flags were innocent of any insulting or even frivolous intention. At the same time, a revue chorus in London was attired in Union Jack handkerchiefs and nothing else—to the public indifference. But the flag, in America, is more than a mere symbol among many others. It is the regimental color of a regiment in which all Americans are enrolled. Its thirteen stripes and forty-eight stars are symbols far better understood than the complicated heraldry of crosses of Saint George, Saint Andrew, and Saint Patrick imposed on each other in a way that only experts understand. . . .

Thus Americanization by ritual is an important and necessary part of the function of the American school. And because it is best carried out in schools, it matters little that the high school curriculum has been so widened that it no longer means a great deal that this boy or that girl has graduated from it—if we are looking for proof of academic achievement. But graduation from high school is reasonable proof that a great deal has been learned about American ways of life, that lessons in practical politics, in organization, in social ease have been learned that could not have been learned in factory or office.

And if the high school seems to devote too much time and money to social life, penalizing the poor boy or girl more than a theoretically less democratic educational system might do, it is thus early impressing an awkward truth on the boy or girl who is both mediocre and poor. It also penalizes the really able boy or girl who is not kept in good enough intellectual training. And if the main business of the school is, in fact, the Americanization of the children of newcomers, the parents of "old American stock" have a good reason (to add to less good ones) for not sending their children to learn what they know already, at the cost of diminishing their chance of learning what they do not know. If English is native to your children and to their home, it is not merely undemocratic to object to having their progress held up and their accent debased by the tone of a high school largely immigrant in composition.

For the task of an American school in many regions is to teach the American language, to enable it to compete with Spanish, with French, with Yiddish, with Polish, with German, with Swedish. Another task is to give, through the language and the literature of the language, a common vocabulary and a common fund of allusion, fable, and sentiment. With a fluid population this has not been easy. And the countless teachers who have labored, pedantically, formally, with complete and erroneous conviction that there were correct standards, have been heroes as important in the mass as was William McGuffey whose *Eclectic Readers* sold over one hundred and twenty million copies and helped to make the Union. The teachers were heroes because, although English won against all its rivals, it was itself going through important changes, in vocabulary, in grammar, in sound becoming the new tongue we are beginning to call American. . . .

Most American parents do not want, or are not able to send their children to anything but public high schools, and the life in such a school is a training in life for America. It may be and often is a training in life *against* Europe. For Europe is the background from which many of the children are reacting and from which they must be delivered if they are to be Americanized. For nearly all immigrants, America is promotion, and this promotion is more clearly felt by their children. The old people may hanker after the old country, but the children—whatever sentimental feelings for their ancestral homes they may have, especially when provoked—are, above all else, anxious to be Americans.

Necessarily something is lost here. The least-common-denominator Americanism of the schools is not a complete substitute for a native culture. What the first-generation American children learn to despise may include elements in their moral diet that are not replaced. A new American whose pride in that promotion involves mere contempt for the habits, what Americans call the "folkways" or "mores," of his parents is not necessarily a good American. So attempts are made to instill pride in the ancestral cultures of the European lands from which the immigrants come. The University of Pittsburgh, located in one of the main melting pots of America, has a set of rooms illustrating the culture of various European countries. In the case of the Greeks, the room may instill adequate pride; in the case of the Scots (if any such need is felt) a shrine of Robert Burns may serve. But, for many of the peasant immigrants, the old country is backward though beloved, while for their children it is merely backward.

Americanization comes not from preservation of Slovak or Italian peasant culture, but from speedy assimilation to "American" culture. And that assimilation may take the form of distinction in anything that the American world obviously values. In the narrow sense of culture, there may even be a temptation to go for those courses that have no immigrant stigma on them. Thus I have been told by an eminent Scandinavian-American that it is difficult to get good students of Scandinavian literature and language at the University of Minnesota, although most of the students have fairly recent Scandinavian connections. They will study French but not Swedish, for "French is not a servant's language." Latin, emblem of functionless "culture," plays something of the same role; it is a symbol of liberation.

Study is not the only way up to Americanization, to acceptation. Sport is another—and one that does the job more dramatically for the newcomers gifted with what it takes to excel in competitive contests, with what is needed to win personal and community and institutional glory.

It is significant that the graduating classes in Muncie High School a generation ago took such mottoes as "Deo duce" and today take mottoes stressing the "Bearcat Spirit," the "Bearcats" being the school basketball team. But a Greek would know where he was at a basketball game uniting boys and girls, parents and civic leaders, in a common passion for competitive achievement. It may be hard on the academic work of the school. . . . but sport, school sport, college sport, does unite the parents, the children, and the community. And sport is rigorously democratic. The sons of Czechs and Poles can score there, can break through the barriers that stand in the way of the children of "Bohunks" and "Polacks." . . .

The cheer leaders, the new "jongleurs de Notre Dame," the "majorettes," shapely young women more or less involved with musical instruments, the massed cheering sections of the students, the massed yelling sections of the alumni—these are the equivalent of the crowds at the great Hellenic festivals in which barbarians were not allowed to compete. The Rose Bowl, the Cotton Bowl, the other intersectional games—these are instruments of national unity, and the provision of such instruments is no mean duty of colleges and universities. It is a religious exercise of a kind a Greek would have understood, however remote it may be from the university as understood by Abelard or Saint Thomas Aquinas or John Harvard.

GEOFFREY GORER
THE DATING RITUAL

Until fairly recently cultural anthropologists have directed their attention exclusively to the study of primitive or "exotic" societies. Geoffrey Gorer's The American People *(1948) is an early attempt "to apply some of the methods and insights of cultural anthropology to a great modern community." In his foreward Gorer described his method as "examining the usual and expected behavior in a number of typical relationships: child to father, child to mother, parents to children, husband and wife, lovers, friends, neighbors, business associates and rivals, employers and employees, majority to minorities, Americans to foreigners, and so on. In its extension and consistency this approach is technically a novel one."*

In 1963 Gorer revised his book, adding a Postscript which commented on changes in the intervening one and a half decades. It is a useful reminder that many of the observations and generalizations included in this volume are limited not only in relating to limited segments of American society but in dealing with isolated stages of a society in constant change.

The passages are reprinted from The American People: A Study in National Character, *by Geoffrey Gorer. By permission of W. W. Norton & Company, Inc. and Barrie and Jenkins Publishers. Copyright 1948 by Geoffrey Gorer. Revised Edition copyright © 1964 by Geoffrey Gorer, pp. 106-117, 258-260.*

In Chapter III, I have viewed the continuous competition between American children of the same age predominantly as it is seen and felt by the parents, and have taken relatively little account of the children's personal involvement. But of course the children are involved in it, most deeply and emotionally involved. For the parents the child's relative success gives the answer to the question: "Have I been a good American parent? Have I produced and equipped a child who can hold his own, make good, amount to something, reach heights which I cannot?" But to the child (and so to the adult) its own success means much more than that. "Am I successful?" comes to mean "Am I loved?" For from the very beginning, the mother's unqualified love and approval have been given to her child in proportion to its success.

By adolescence most Americans have inextricably confused the two ideas: to be successful is to be loved, to be loved is to be successful. This confusion is even given a quasi-theological sanction, derived from the puritanism of New England as diffused by the schoolteachers: worldly success is an outward and visible sign of the love of God, of Providence; to be a failure signifies that one is unloved by God, that one has sinned, or, at the least, has not tried hard enough.

To gain one's mother's love, the prototype of all future love, it is not necessary that one should show love in return; one is loved for one's accomplishments vis-à-vis one's age mates, not in the first place for one's attitude and behavior toward one's mother. Love in America therefore tends to have a nonreciprocal quality: to be loved it is not necessary to love in return, but rather to be worthy of love. This of course does not mean that mutual love is absent in America, nor even rarer than in other countries, but there is superadded this nonsymmetrical component, which can only become symmetrical by identification, by conceiving the loved one to be, as it were, part of oneself, as worthy of love as oneself. . . .

The presence, the attention, the admiration of other people thus becomes for Americans a necessary component to their self-esteem, demanded with a feeling of far greater psychological urgency than is usual in other countries. This gives a special tone to the social relationships of Americans with their fellows (with the exception, on occasion, of marital and parental relationships): they are, in the first instance, devices by which a person's self-esteem is maintained and enhanced. They can be considered exploitative, but this exploitation is nearly always mutual: "I will assure you that you are a success if you will assure me that I am" might be the unspoken contract under which two people begin a mutual relationship. The most satisfying form of this assurance is not given by direct flattery or commendation (this by itself is suspect as a device to exploit the other) but by love, or at least the concentrated, exclusive attention which shows that one is worthy of interest and esteem.

It is only against this psychological background that what is probably the most singular feature of American social life can be understood: the "dating" which occupies so much of nearly every American's leisure time from before adolescence until betrothal, and which for many continues even after, if separation or satiety lessens the satisfactions to be derived from the betrothed, or if excessive individual anxiety demands more reassurance than betrothed or spouse or lover can give. "Dating" is idiosyncratic in many ways, but especially so in that it uses the language and gestures of courtship and love-making, without necessarily implying the reality of either. The overt differences of behavior which distinguish "dating" from courtship are so slight as to be barely perceptible; yet only in rare cases, and those involving unbalanced people, does confusion result—when both partners are American. "Dating" is a highly patterned activity or group of activities, comparable in some ways to a formal dance, in others to a very complicated competitive game; it is comparable to a dance in that the gestures employed do not have the significance they would have in other settings (witness the bows and curtsies of the minuet, the close embrace of the waltz and later ballroom dances); but it is more nearly comparable to such a competitive game as chess, in which the rules are known to, and observed by, both parties, but in which each move, after the opening gambit, is a response to the previous move of the other player. As in dances and games, the activity is felt to be enjoyable and rewarding for its own sake, and the more enjoyable the more nearly the partners or players are matched in skill and other necessary qualifications. The comparison with competitive games, such as chess, can be carried further; both partners must play with concentration and seriousness, using all their ingenuity, within the accepted rules, to be the victor; apart from the pleasure of the game, there is also the pleasant enhancement to one's self-esteem that winning the game provides. There is one aspect, however, in which the comparison of "dating" to chess breaks down; in a successful date there should not be a loser; both parties should feel their self-esteem, their assurance, enhanced.

As far as I know, no other society has been recorded which has developed a similar institutionalized type of behavior for its young people. A number of societies, of which the Samoans and the Trobrianders are well-known examples, allow for a period of sexual license and experiment before betrothal and marriage; but these are, and are meant to be, years of sensual and sexual satisfaction, sought for their own sake. In American "dating" sensual and sexual satisfactions may play a part (though this is by no means necessary) as counters in the game, but they are not the object of the exercise; the object of the exercise is enhanced self-esteem, assurance that one is lovable, and therefore a success.

A further complication arises from the fact that the words and gestures of love are regularly employed in "dating" without either party taking them for anything but counterfeit, moves in the game; and yet Americans believe very deeply and passionately in love (a concept not shared by the Samoans, nor the Trobrianders, nor many of the peoples of whom we have adequate studies). It is difficult to find comparisons for thus using frivolously in one context words and gestures which may be of the greatest importance in another. A very far-fetched one could be derived from the game of chess. In a period of monarchical passions and court intrigue "Your queen is captured" or "Your king is threatened" could have completely different significance according to the settings in which the phrases were used.

There is, finally, the complication that "dating," employing and being known to employ the words and gestures of love-making, is admitted and abetted by parents and teachers who, many of them, hold the puritan attitudes toward sex and the pleasures of the body, even though these attitudes do not seem to be held by most of the younger generation. . . .

In a "date" the opening move, at least overtly, should come from the boy, in the form of an invitation to the girl to spend the evening in his company. The basis of selection is somewhat different for the boy and for the girl. For the girl the object is to have as many invitations as possible, so that she can choose among them the partner whom she thinks can give her the best time, or who will be the most fun to compete with; for the boy the object is to have as his partner the girl who is most admired and most sought after by his companions and fellow rivals. A girl who only got a single invitation to an important social event (say a commencement dance), even though it was from the most desirable boy, the captain of the football team, would be doubtfully pleased (this, of course, on condition that they are not courting); a boy whose invitation is accepted by the local "belle" in similar circumstances has already gained a major social triumph. Consequently, participation in the "dating" pattern is somewhat different for the two sexes: all boys can and should take part in it, the level to which they aspire being dependent on their qualifications; but only the most successful and popular girls in each set do so fully, the rest having to be content with a steady boy friend, or even the companionship of a fellow unfortunate.

Unless an American boy is very poor, very maladjusted, or for some reason almost totally excluded from social life, "dating" and earning money for "dates" will occupy the greater part of his leisure time from early adolescence until betrothal. The social pressure toward doing so is very great. Thus in a typical Midwestern college fraternity the senior members insisted that the juniors have at least three "dates" a week; and further that these "dates" should be with girls who did honor to the fraternity, and, barring betrothal, should not be too frequently with the same girl. Such open control and supervision is unusual, but few Americans would quarrel with the standard of behavior demanded.

The experience of girls is much less uniform, since they are dependent on the boys' invitations, and the boys will invite the most popular girls obtainable. As a consequence some girls will have almost all their time taken up by "dates," while others have at most an occasional one, and many others drop out of the competition altogether until betrothal. . . .

The "date" starts as an invitation from a young man to a girl for an evening's public entertainment, typically at his expense, though since the depression girls occasionally pay their share. The entertainment offered depends on the young man's means and aspirations, and the locality; but it is in a public place always, and nearly always includes eating food together, the food being anything from an ice-cream soda at the local drugstore to the most elaborate and expensive meal that the locality can provide. Besides the food, the most usual entertainment is dancing—the place of the dance ranging anywhere from the cheap roadside café with a jukebox to the most expensive cabaret or country club. The male (the "escort") should call for the girl in a car (unless he be particularly young or poor) and should take her back in the car. If the entertainment proposed is of a formal or expensive nature, the man should provide a corsage—flowers for the girl to wear on her dress or in her hair.

The corsage is the first sign of the man's estimate of his partner for the evening, partly through the expense of the flowers, and partly according to the extent to which they are particularly suited to the girl's appearance, personality, or costume. Every item of the subsequent entertainment gives further signs; the relative amount of money spent is important for the girl's self-esteem, and not in itself.

"Showing the girl a good time" is the essential background for a "date," but it is not its object, as far as the man is concerned; its object is to get the girl to prove that he is worthy of love, and therefore a success. In some cases superior efficiency in dancing will elicit the necessary signs of approval; but typically, and not unexpectedly, they are elicited by talk. Once again, the importance of words is paramount.

Since, on first "dates" the pair are normally comparative strangers to one another, a certain amount of autobiography is necessary in the hopes of establishing some common interest or experience, at the least to prove that one is worthy of the other's attention. These autobiographies, however, differ at most in emphasis, in tone of voice, from those which should accompany any American meeting between strangers. What distinguishes the "date" from other conversation is a mixture of persiflage, flattery, wit and love-making which was formerly called a "line" but which each generation dubs with a new name.

The "line" is an individual variation of a commonly accepted pattern which is considered to be representative of a facet of a man's personality. Most men are articulately self-conscious about their "lines" and can describe them with ease; they are constantly practiced and improved with ever differing partners. The object of the "line" is to entertain, amuse, and captivate the girl, but there is no deep emotional involvement; it is a game of skill.

The girl's skill consists in parrying the "line" without discouraging her partner or becoming emotionally involved herself. To the extent that she falls for the "line" she is a loser in this intricate game; but if she discourages her partner so much that he does not request a subsequent "date" in the near future she is equally a loser. To remain the winner, she must make the nicest discriminations between yielding and rigidity.

The man scores to the extent that he is able to get more favors from the girl than his rivals, real or supposed, would be able to do. The proving time is the return journey from the place of public entertainment to the girl's home. A good-night kiss is almost the minimum repayment for an evening's entertainment; but how much more depends on the enterprise of the man, the self-assurance of the woman, and the number of "dates" the pair have had together. This love-making is still emotionally uninvolved; it is still part of the game, though the gestures and intimacies and language are identical with true love-making; it is not, save most rarely, an attempt at seduction; and the satisfactions sought are not, in the first instance, sensual but self-regarding. The man should demonstrate his enterprise and prove that he is worthy to be loved by pressing for ever further favors; but the girl who yields too much, or too easily, may well be a disappointment, in exactly the same way as too easy a victory in tennis or chess may be a disappointment.

It is usual—but not essential—that intimacies should increase with each successive "date" with the same partner, up to the threshold of, but seldom including, actual intercourse. The contest continues in these later phases, though slightly less articulately; the victor is the one who makes the other lose self-control without losing it him (or her) self.

It must be repeated that the goal of "dating" is not in the first place sexual satisfaction. An "easy lay" is not a good "date," and conversely. Apart from professional or semiprofessional prostitutes, there are in most groups girls who create for themselves an illusion of popularity by promiscuity. Their telephone numbers may get bandied about, but they are not the girls who get the orchid corsages, or get taken to the ringside tables at the best restaurants. It would be a paradox, but not too great a one, to say that the converse was more nearly true: that the ideal date is one in which both partners are so popular, so skilled, and so self-assured that the result is a draw. . . .

The biggest superficial change in American life since I wrote *The American People* is the greatly decreased importance of dating behavior for adolescents and young adults. This has now been typically transformed into pre-adolescent behavior, suitable for youngsters in their earliest teens, the rehearsal for the social world of physiological maturity. Very shortly after this is attained, the prevailing pattern is "going steady," the boy and girl spending all their leisure time in one another's company, behaving as if they were betrothed; such practices as the "stag line" or "cutting in" at formal dances are said to be falling into desuetude. In this more concentrated relationship, the boy's aim is sexual intercourse, rather than the lesser intimacies of "heavy petting"; and, it would appear, he is frequently gratified, though the girl may retain some symbolic virginity (such as not undressing completely) until she is certain of marriage. Although some lip-service is paid to female chastity, especially among the church-going middle classes, there are no institutions left to help the girls protect themselves; indeed one of the reasons for young men attending a church of their selection is that this is one of the best situations in which to meet desirable girls. Outside the South, men are not responsible for watching over their womenfolk's chastity; brothers have no responsibility towards their sisters; and only a minority of parents will take the risk of having their daughter become unpopular and neglected by being more severe and circumspect than their neighbors.

A further hazard is raised by the fact that doctors and birth-control centers (in those states where they are not forbidden) conceive themselves to be guardians of morality, or fear to be accused of promoting immorality (if not of "communist" behavior) and therefore will not give advice nor fit appliances for girls who are neither betrothed nor married. Though this can be circumvented by purchasing a cheap wedding ring at any five-and-ten store before visiting the doctor, many girls, particularly those of the most admirable character, have a distaste for acting such a lie. Consequently early pregnancies and early marriages are becoming increasingly frequent; young people may be the parents of two or three children before they have completed their education. They will typically continue their university studies until they have got a B.A., for a college degree is being increasingly demanded for ever more unacademic jobs and positions; but with such domestic distractions and responsibilities it is unlikely that the academic work will be of much depth or originality. Intellectual adventurousness and early parenthood would seem to be mutually incompatible.

ROBERT JUNGK
THE PIED PIPER

Mass television and mass advertising are two closely related phenomena that are commonly associated with American life. In few

other countries are both allowed the extent of uninhibited proliferation
they enjoy in the United States. In few other countries have they been
allowed to invade the privacy of the individual and the family as in
the United States.

Robert Jungk's brief look at commercial television and the Ameri-
can family in Tomorrow Is Already Here *(London, 1954) opens up*
frightening perspectives for anyone who has not lost the ability to see
the dangers inherent in our western civilization. It is taken from pp.
209-212. Copyright © by Scherz Verlag Bern-München-Wien.

"You must excuse Johnnie," said the lady of the house as we sat
down to dinner, "he doesn't eat with us in the evenings any longer
but picnics in the corral with the other cowboys." She tried to smile
and her husband made an effort to sketch a discreet "Hiyooo" in
the cowboy style. Then we spooned our soup in silence. The parents
had at first been a trifle relieved when their eight-year-old son stopped
taking his evening meal with them. At last they could speak freely
again at table on any topic they chose, were not interrupted by endless
questions, did not have to exhort Junior to eat nicely. But now they
had begun to miss him.

"Do excuse me," said the lady of the house again, "I must just
see whether Johnnie is drinking his milk." With that she vanished
into the next room. As she opened the door the thud of hoofbeats
came in to us for a moment, and the shrill mechanical tones of a
musical accompaniment. "There was nothing else to do," explained
the host; "the child was simply not to be held once the 'Hoppy Show'
had begun. Slid about on his chair, stuffed down the last mouthfuls
in a hurry, or else left half his plate untouched, anything to get back
quickly to his television set. Now we serve his meal in there on the
folding table. He eats and watches. Imagines with all his soul he is
a regular cowboy and greets me when I come home with his silver
revolver drawn and an affectionate 'Hands up'."

Johnnie's case is typical of what happened to innumberable American families when the television set entered their lives. It seemed as
though the Pied Piper, once followed by the children of Hamelin on
the Weser, had been resurrected in the United States. Almost without
exception the children of America have followed the call of this newcomer. While grown-ups, as soon as the charm of novelty has worn

off, find a place for the T.V. set among other minor interests and amusements, the boys and girls are insatiable. Children between the ages of three and thirteen spend many hours daily before the little magic screen that offers them stories without cease, adventures, jokes, thrilling detective yarns, and in between salvoes of advertising slogans.

The television set gratifies the children's natural hunger for adventure far more thoroughly than the picture-book has ever been able to do. It is a tireless story-teller which always has time. Even three or four-year-olds are able to perform the simple act of snapping on the current. No longer do they need to acquire reality painstakingly, bit by bit: it is already there, in the middle of the parental living-room.

Like most of what will later be offered for sale to these young Americans, whether in the form of food, music, or the theatre, it is selected, prepared and put up in potted form by others. The perfect consumer, who is dependent on the creativeness and taste of an ever-decreasing number of producers, is formed at an early age, before experiences of his own have been able to affect his character, or his own fantasies to unfold in a normal way.

"The children no longer do their homework," complain the teachers. "It's impossible to get Junior to go to sleep," say the mothers. And the fathers are horrified at the language of their offspring. "The devil take it," raged an eight-year-old, as reported by the television critic of the *New York Times*. "If I have to go along to see Grandpa someone will bear the consequences." Thereupon he ran the water-tap and mixed a deadly poisonous drink as he had seen done in the television serial *Suspense*. A small girl passing a public house with her father, chirped what she had learned from the T.V. advertisements: "Ask for Ballantyne's beer."

When I heard these stories for the first time I laughed, as one does at the sayings of children. Only when I saw children in a West Hollywood street singing advertising couplets set to music in place of the old nursery songs, and when a few weeks later in the gigantic new Van Nuys Supermarket I heard a small boy in a black cowboy suit urge his mother: "Please Mummy, buy only 'Barbara Ann' bread. Hoppy says it makes him strong," did I begin to understand the game: through television the advertising bureaus had turned millions of little boys and girls into voluntary agents. The American citizen, hardened against propaganda, may ignore certain enticements. But when a child's voice pleads, who—particularly in America—can resist?

The discovery of the child market is not of recent date. The promoters of the breakfast foods sold in variegated cartons built up their business on the children's good will. The firm which accompanied its packages with the prettiest prizes (or which offered them on receipt of the carton lid) could count on the largest youthful clientele. Thus "Wheaties" shortly after the launching of the first atomic bomb outstripped all its rivals by promising its young customers an "atom ring with radioactive substance".

But these things were a mere prelude to the greatest spectacle of child mass hysteria since the distant days of the Children's Crusade. It dated from the rise of an old cowboy actor, Bill Boyd, in the television role of the virtuous Hopalong Cassidy, to become the idol of the youth of an entire nation. In reality Hoppy was neither so virtuous nor so brave as he was represented. He had long led a notoriously wild life and hated nothing so much as locomotion on the back of a horse. But that was of no importance: the fairy-tale tellers had found in him a mythical hero of stature and harnessed him to their various advertising chariots in a way they had never before used a living person.

Not only were a million cowboy suits (at $20 to $45) sold in a few months, but also nearly as many pistols (50 cents to $5.50), spurs ($2 to $4), knives (60 cents to $7), and riding-boots ($4 to $9). And as the Hoppy-enthusiasm continued to grow, other producers of the most varied objects, by no means necessarily for the use of the young, were seized with Hoppy-madness. In return for five per cent of the selling price Hopalong Cassidy was prepared to let himself be made patron of savings-banks, bakery firms, necktie-designers, watchmakers, chocolate factories and brands of soap. About five hundred various Hoppy products appeared on the market and were purchased by the parents of twenty-five million children.

That went on until the Hoppy symbol, through a carefully planned and cleverly carried out counter-attack by a group of advertising people, gradually lost ground. A radio programme with the Space Cadet Tom Corbett as its hero, a sort of interplanetary cowboy who disposed of his opponent with the death-ray pistol, began its triumphal journey on television.

I saw the downfall of Hoppy and the rise of his rival foreshadowed on the evening I had to dine with my Boston hosts without the presence of Johnnie. To his father's astonishment the hostess returned from the living-room, from which emerged the sound of Hoppy's gallop, not alone as we had expected, but accompanied by her offspring, a pale little boy who remarked by way of explanation: "That guy is beginning to bore me."

A month later his father had bought him a space-suit ($24.50), an antidote against cosmic rays (sweets at 60 cents) and a pair of anti-gravity shoes ($7.20). And when he came home his son received him with a loud "Hands pu"—which is not much more difficult to pronounce than "Hands up" and is well known to mean the same in the language of Mars—as he pointed the ray-gun ($3.98) at him. Papa obeyed this order without delay, and before the raised arms had time to descend his Johnnie had already vanished to consume his supper aboard a space rocket.

VI. AMERICA ABROAD

As a super power the United States has an impact not only on other nations but on the daily lives of individuals the world over. An American election is by many felt to be of greater concern than their own national elections. This is a fairly recent state of affairs. The American influence was not much felt outside of the Western Hemisphere, with the exception of occasional excursions across the Pacific and President Wilson's brief and aborted European Crusade, until the United States entered the Second World War. The presidency of Franklin D. Roosevelt, as Roy Jenkins, former member of the British Cabinet, put it recently, "was the decisive stage in the evolution of the United States to full world power, and of Washington . . . to a position as near to the political capital of the world as has ever been occupied by any city since the fall of imperial Rome" (*Afternoon on the Potomac: A British View of America's Changing Position in the World,* 1972).

The title of John Strachey's book, from which the first of the following excerpts is taken, *Hope in America* (1938), reflects the attitude of intellectuals and liberals as well as socialists to the rising power of the United States in the early decades of the twentieth century.

Has American capitalism, as Strachey hoped, ceased its imperialistic search for foreign markets since the Spanish-American War? Has America lived up to Strachey's other liberal-democratic hopes since 1938? What are the benefits and dangers of America's position as "world policeman?" Does America "enjoy the highest possible moral authority in the world?" Why is America disliked abroad? Why does America, the world's leading democracy, openly or covertly support some of the world's leading dictatorships? What are the dangers—for America and for the "invaded" country—of American ownership of foreign businesses?

JOHN STRACHEY
AMERICA'S CHOICE

In a Europe where Fascism was on the march and where statesmen like Neville Chamberlain, the British Prime Minister, seemed blissfully unaware of the menace, the European Left and Center looked to the United States of Franklin D. Roosevelt and the New Deal. John Strachey (1901-   ), a British Marxist, had written several analyses of capitalism, socialism and The Menace of Fascism *(1933). His study of the New Deal converted him from revolutionary Marxism to a reformist approach and a belief in the importance of the American experiment for the future of the world. His analysis of the relationship between capitalism and imperialism may still be relevant for a consideration of American foreign policy today. "America's Choice" is taken from his* Hope in America *(New York: Modern Age Books, 1938), pp. 115-123, where he evaluated the achievements of the New Deal and suggested the direction further reforms should take.*

Now America is not so acutely or so immediately threatened by the reappearance of German imperialism as are the nations of Western Europe, such as Britain and France. All the same, I believe that she errs if she thinks that she is not threatened.

I said in the first chapter of this book that a Fascist Europe, a Europe under the domination of German imperialism, that is to say, would be not only a ghastly but also a very strong thing. It would be a continent launched on a career of world conquest. No nation, however strong or however distant, would be free from its menace. Hence it would seem to me that the American people, strictly for their own sakes, would be well advised to take part in the movement of all free peoples to stop the Fascists before they become so strong that civilization will be almost wrecked in the job of stopping them.

I am not disposed, however, to say much more about this question than that one sentence. For so long as the British government pursues its present policy of connivance in, and condonation of, every act of Fascist aggression in the world, it is almost impossible for any Britisher to ask the American people to aid the British people in the task of stopping Fascist aggression before it is too late. It is the duty of Britain to set the example, for Britain is nearer the aggressor and more immediately threatened.

The British governing class, I notice, while refusing itself to make the slightest move to stop the Fascist aggressors; while indeed aiding and abetting their aggression in every way, at the same time is beginning to start a propaganda in America by which it is seeking to persuade the American people that they must come and help the British if, in spite of all Britain's concessions to the Fascists, Britain is attacked. This propaganda shows, on the one hand, that the British governing class, in spite of all it has done for the Fascist aggressors, knows that they may at any moment turn upon it. And, on the other hand, it shows a very poor opinion of the intelligence of the American people. Nothing seems to me more undignified or more hypocritical than this request of the British governing class to the American people to save democracy, world peace, etc., etc., while the British government is every day betraying these very things.

I am sure that the American people will make up their own minds as to what America's world policy should be. If they decide, as I believe they will in the end, that they must join hands with every people whose intent it is to resist Fascist aggression, then they will do so strictly because they see that it is in their own interest, and for their own safety, to do so. It will not be until we get a progressive government in Britain that we shall be able to follow such a good example on the part of America.

There are, however, people who say that all this talk of resisting Fascist aggression is wrong; that what we ought to do is to give the Fascists what they want; to hand over colonies to the Fascists; to share the markets of the world with them.

Now there are two overwhelming objections to such a course.

First, people who talk like this are really regarding colonies as if they were pawns in some complex game of international chess. But colonies are whole countries inhabited by whole peoples. In some cases, such as India, the greatest of all colonies, they are subcontinents, inhabited by dozens of different peoples. What possible right have we to hand over such countries, with their peoples, to the Fascists? . . .

But there is a deeper reason than this for rejecting the idea of trying to buy off the Fascist aggressors with a few colonies. This whole idea really accepts the imperialist answer to our basic question of who is to buy the goods. It is based on the idea that states can live only if they acquire great chunks of the world as their exclusive markets. In other words, it is based upon an acceptance of the existing economic system. Is it not easy to see, however, that there is no way out for the world as long as you accept this basis? *Peace does not lie down this road.* However you shuffle round the available colonies between the various empires, there will always be some empires which will have too few markets to be able to exist. And these empires will be driven outward in the attempt to acquire more. There are not anything like enough colonies, or potential colonies, to go round. The empires are growing in number. Their productive capacity is expanding rapidly. They cannot, or will not, give their peoples any more purchasing power; hence their need for markets becomes ever more desperate.

It is utterly impossible to solve the question by any reshuffle of those markets which are available. The only way it can be solved is by giving the populations of the empires themselves enough purchasing power to buy the goods. And this process, although it can be, and ought to be, begun along the lines of Mr. Roosevelt's distributions of purchasing power, can only be finally successful if the ownership of the capital of the country is itself changed.

But what about America in all this? Why, the reader will ask, have not the American capitalists long before this been driven to give the imperialist answer to the question of who is to buy the goods? Well, of course, to some extent they have. About thirty or forty years ago American capitalism appeared to have embarked on the usual imperialist course. She was acquiring what were colonies, in fact if not in name, in the Pacific, in Central and South America, etc., etc. She brushed aside in a typical, if small, imperialist war the feeble resistance of Spain. America seemed to have her foot planted on the imperialist course.

But then, in the postwar period, American capitalism passed into its last, but greatest period of internal expansion. American capitalism had so vast a home country that it was able to enjoy one last great boom in developing its own home territories. To some extent this arrested the course of American imperialism. In the postwar period America acquired no new colonies and, on the whole, became less interested even in those which she had. She invented, however, a new kind of economic expansion into the outside world. Without actually attempting to annex any new territories, she made enormous loans of American capital to all sorts of foreign countries, from Germany on the one hand to the South American republics on the other, to say nothing of the money she had lent to the British and other allied countries during the war. No doubt the boom of the twenties could not have been so big, or have lasted so long, without this new form of economic expansion into the outside world.

The British capitalists, however, would have said that this was a very risky thing to do. They would have said that if you lent money to states which you did not take the precaution to conquer and annex, it would probably mean that you would lose your money in the end. For it would mean that you had not the power to make your debtors pay.

And so, as a matter of fact, it turned out. This new kind of American economic expansion, which did not carry the full imperialist implications with it, proved a failure. America did lose a very high proportion indeed of all the money she had lent abroad.

The result has been a very strong reaction among the American people against any attempt to solve their economic difficulties by means of economic expansion into other countries, and against Imperialism in particular. To a British observer especially, it is extremely remarkable how, during all the acute economic difficulties of the last ten years, hardly anyone in America has attempted or suggested a new imperialist drive as the solution. America seems to have turned her back on the imperialist road; she seems to have her feet planted more or less firmly upon the road which leads to solving the problem by means of making her own population the ultimate market for her goods.

We have followed out Mr. Roosevelt's extensive and courageous attempt to solve the problem along these progressive lines. But we have also seen how much there remains to be done before the problem is solved. This attempt was bound to encounter terrific opposition from the capitalist class; for the question of who is to buy the goods can be solved along these lines only at the expense of the capitalists

We come to this conclusion then. If the present American attempt to answer the question of who is to buy the goods in the progressive way, if the attempt to equip the American people with adequate purchasing power—no matter whose interests and whose prejudices stand in the way—were to fail, then America would inevitably be forced back onto the imperialist road. If the forces which at present center round Mr. Roosevelt were to be defeated, if the whole progressive attempt to distribute purchasing power and to begin the modification of capitalism in America were discredited and defeated, then the only remaining possibility for the American people would be the path of imperialist conquest.

The instinctive opposition of nearly all Americans to such a course would probably necessitate the imposition of some kind of fascist tyranny upon them in order to make it possible for the leading bankers and capitalists to take them down the imperialist road. At the same time one must remember that the first step along the imperialist road can be made insidiously attractive. This first step usually consists in the inauguration of a gigantic program of armaments. Now it is perfectly true that armaments, which in their economic effects are only a particular kind of public works, will act as a stimulus upon the economic system. Hence they may look attractive to many people who would otherwise be strongly opposed to any tendency toward imperialism. Still I do not believe that the American people could be got beyond this first step of their own free will; some kind of fascism would be needed to get them any farther. But if that happened, if the American people were enslaved, we should get by far the most powerful fascist, imperialist capitalism which the world had ever seen, rushing out for a struggle with the Fascist capitalisms of Europe to dominate the world.

The German Nazis would wake up to the unpleasant fact that two could play at their game of attempting to solve the problem by imperialist expansion! They would meet in an American fascist capitalism a rival more formidable than themselves. But in the ensuing struggle we should all be killed!

It seems to me, therefore, that the fate of the whole world is bound up with the success of the American people in their present attempt to solve their problem along the progressive lines of equipping themselves with sufficient purchasing power to keep themselves in employment.

SALAVADOR DE MADARIAGA
THE KEY NATION FOR THE FUTURE OF THE WORLD

Salvador de Madariaga (1886-) is a distinguished Spanish scholar who served the Spanish Republic as a diplomat in the early 1930s. Although he did not take part in the Civil War, he has lived in exile since Franco came to power. His humanistic democratic faith is expressed in Latin America Between the Eagle and the Bear, *by Salvador de Madariaga. © 1962 by Salvador de Madariaga. Excerpted and reprinted by permission of Praeger Publishers, Inc., New York, where his "hope in America" is sobered by his intimate knowledge of American imperialism in Latin America. The following extract is taken from the beginning of his third chapter, "The American Aspect," pp. 66-75.*

When he writes about Guatemala Madariaga shows little sympathy for what he calls the "anti-Americanism" of Juan José Arévalo (pp. 88-95); but his own "pro-Americanism" makes his critique of United States imperialism all the more poignant.

Before coming closer to the subject of the relations between the United States and Latin America, it is indispensable to place the subject as a whole in a world perspective. Any views on any international subject that do not set themselves into our contemporary scheme of things, no matter how well founded they may be on the ideas or emotions of the persons concerned, are bound to lead to frustration and failure. Now the scheme of things in which we live happens to make of the United States the key nation for the future of the world.

It must be owned that this paramount consideration is far too often overlooked by critics of the United States; indeed, is it not too often neglected by the United States herself? It is therefore imperative to recall the fact as forcibly as possible from the very outset of our enquiry, and in the process, to define and clarify it to the best of our ability. The scheme of things in which we are living presents a number of features which must be clearly, if briefly, sketched.

Mostly owing to the progress of applied science, the world is rapidly evolving towards a world community, may indeed be said to be already a community. News, views, emotions, travel throughout the planet in less time than it took them to move across a Greek *agora*; and men fly round the world in much less time than Julius Caesar or indeed Napoleon took to ride across France. Since the world is already one community, it must, sooner or later, be governed as one commonwealth. But for a community to become a commonwealth it must be unanimous on a minimum of ideas about itself and the world.

This degree of unanimity is for the present unattainable because there is a Great Schism on. The evolution of the European spirit inspired on its intellectual side by Socrates, on its affective side by Christ, is challenged by a heretical sect which denies both truth and love for the sake of a theoretical construction of the society of men which men, when free, reject. This Schism is unbridgeable.

The world commonwealth can therefore be built only if either the one or the other of the policical philosophies facing each other eliminates its adversary. The liberal philosophy relies on discussion, free trial and error, and spontaneous agreement. The communist philosophy relies on dogma and police force. Logically, therefore, the communist philosophy should spread by the sword—and so it does whenever it can.

Expansion by force, however, has become an impossibility owing to the devastating power of modern weapons. This circumstance has fundamentally altered the character of the political evolution of the world from a community to a commonwealth; for it has determined a movement from arms to ideas, from force to public opinion, and therefore, in an essential and inescapable way, from the communist to the liberal way of doing things. It means, therefore, that the Communist Party must henceforth reserve its genuine methods—fraud and force, power and oppression—for carefully circumscribed, local operations, while carrying on its world fight by means of the essentially liberal weapons which are arguments, ideas, discussion, conviction.

This, however, presupposes that the deterrent effect of the modern means of destruction is effective on the communist leadership. For such a thing to happen, it has been indispensable for the United States to organize the superb system of defence which she has erected out of almost nothing since the communist aggression on Korea awoke the nation to the danger. Those who remember what the armed forces of America were in 1898, or even in 1916, will no doubt feel the deepest admiration, and gratitude, for such an achievement. And this is the first of the two reasons why no view on international relations is worth expressing today that does not take into consideration the paramount importance of the United States for the very existence and future of man and his works on earth.

Nevertheless, it is only the first, and though so weighty, not perhaps the weightier of the two. For the very success of the American defence system neutralizes so to speak the military, or defence, aspect of things altogether and causes a shift of stress from force to opinion in the factors that determine world policy. Now this shift of stress should warm the heart of every democrat, because it means an inevitable evolution from autocracy to democracy, since autocracy is based on force and democracy on opinion.

It follows that the aim of the war—"Which war?" you ask. "Is there a war on?" Of course there is. A war is a conflict of wills. The Great Schism mentioned above generates a conflict of wills. This conflict bears on how the world community is going to evolve into a world commonwealth: by means of a resigned conformity enforced from above by one part, one secret police and one army, or through a unanimity gradually blossoming from its roots, like the unanimous harmony of a garden. May I now return to my line of argument? The aim of this war must therefore be to conquer public opinion by an honest and sincere debate on the part of the West, by every possible measure and device on the part of the communist world.

This means that henceforth the struggle will be less and less one of force (granted a strong defence to neutralize the adversary), more and more one of authority. That (relatively recent) habit of describing dictatorial, tyrannical, despotic régimes as authoritarian must be rejected as singularly unfortunate. Authority is the very opposite of force. Force is a bully that steals obedience. Authority is given acquiescence out of the abundance of the heart. The power of the Queen of England is almost nil. Her authority is immense. The power of Franco is immense. His authority is nil.

Fortunately for us, the world is evolving in such a way that its affairs are being solved more and more by authority, less and less by force. It follows that *it is of primary importance for the very survi-*

val of our civilization that the United States enjoy the highest possible moral authority in the world.

And that is my second point, far more weighty (I do believe) than the first. We all, free citizens of the still free part of the world, owe the United States admiration and gratitude for the magnificent achievement of her watch and defence system; but we also owe the United States all the support it is in our power to offer in order to uphold in the world her moral authority, without which the cold war must be lost.

It is in this spirit that the following pages have been written.

It may safely be said that no country in man's history has reached a peak of moral authority as high as that the United States possessed at the time of the Marshall Plan. Moral authority, not prestige. The world would be a better place if the word *prestige* were banished from its vocabulary, and what it represents from its thoughts and attitudes. Prestige is a form of national vanity. It is a poor substitute for moral authority.

At the time of the Marshall Plan the United States reached an historical summit of moral authority. As President Eisenhower left the public stage, the moral authority of the United States was at its lowest ebb. Let American public opinion be in no doubt about it, misinformed though it often is on these matters. Information is not easy. (There is the language difficulty, the courtesy of the foreigner asked, who would hesitate to offend, may be other similar obstacles.) The fact is that in wider and wider circles Americans are more and more disliked and, what is still worse, less and less respected.

The causes are many and complex, but may be classed into three orders: spontaneous-unfair; induced-unfair; spontaneous-fair.

The first order of causes of the widespread dislike of Americans is mostly due to the darker side of human nature: ingratitude, envy, pride. Man being what he is, this saturnine reaction of the recipients of favour to the jovial giver can no more be avoided than the cool, dark shadows cast by the sunlit walls on the corners where the dank air rots and stinks. We just pass on.

The induced-unfair order of causes for dislike of the Americans is due to the ever active militancy of the Communist Party. . . . It is perfectly able, if need be, to work on nothing as raw material, as was shown in the now forgotten campaign started by Chinese communists on the use of bacteriological weapons in the Korean war. But, of course, it works better on good genuine raw material. And that is why the third order of causes is twice to be regretted.

This in its turn splits into two sub-orders; the first more superficial and more irritating; the second, more profound and, in the long run, far more dangerous. The first can be shortly described as *friction*. It is composed of all the small occasions for trouble and strife that arise in the constant rubbing against each other of human surfaces of different texture. American soldiers and civilians are nowadays present, settled, active, in so many places in the world, under so many climates and civilizations that it would be a miracle if at least a good handful of incidents did not occur every hour on the planet; and an even more wonderful miracle if in these inevitable incidents the Americans were always right and the natives wrong. The responsibility of the American government in endeavouring to reduce this kind of friction to a minimum is obvious; but the subject need not detain us any longer.

The second sub-order of spontaneous-fair criticism of the United States is, however, far more serious. It poses the fundamental question: War, yes. But for the defence of what? When the Marshall Plan was offered to Europe, the world was still resonant with the answer to that question: Liberty! And our ears still remember the sound of that word vibrating in the voice of Roosevelt and in the voice of Churchill. That word was not to be heard again until on 20th January, 1961, it rang over the whole earth with the voice of Kennedy.

The nation that had led the world in her struggle for liberty had gradually become the friend and ally of every dictator in the world, every nation-breaker who had gangstered his way to power and simply laughed outright at liberty and democracy and the rest of it. Forgetting that the stress had shifted from arms to faith, from conquering to convincing, the nation that had given forth Jefferson and Lincoln embraced Franco and Tito for the sake of bases and harbours; and grew so discreet about the freedom of Eastern Europe that the world began to wonder whether Washington and London were not thinking of letting Eastern Europe go for good for the sake of "peace". Unable to rally its friends for lack of a rallying cry and a banner, the West grew disgruntled, disorientated and divided. Power-policy reappeared, hardly rejuvenated by a laborious face-lift; and the free world verbal currency was debased to such an extent that the word *peace* uttered by Khrushchev was accepted as good money, and John Foster Dulles left Madrid declaring that he and Franco had studied matters of common interest for the *free* nations of the world. Faced with such deliberate counterfeiting carried out openly by its own verbal bankers, the public opinion of the world ceased to grant them any credit. When Eisenhower left office (not without sending a cordial message of thanks to Franco "for his services to world peace") no one anywhere believed any longer in anything. Least of all in the United States.

Since our chief aim must be to restore the moral authority of the United States, it is now our task to endeavour to find out how and why it was lost. The loss of moral authority came about for a complex system of reasons which may well repay a moment of attention. It originated in the Pentagon, owing to the professional pressure to stress the needs of the defence apparatus. Such a stressing was, of course, not merely legitimate but indispensable. It should have been the task of the State Department and the White House to have pointed out that, since the world was nowadays governed predominantly by public opinion, the defence apparatus should be conceived in such a way as not to impair the authority of the United States or the faith of the West in its own cause.

The solution adopted was the very worst. It consisted in seeking the alliance of anyone who suited the defence apparatus no matter how injurious this alliance might be to the faith and morale of the West, and *to pretend that the new ally was all right,* i.e., to fool the people. In so doing the spokesmen of the American people forgot that Lincoln's famous utterance now rules the whole world community: "You can fool some of the people all the time, and all the people some of the time; but you cannot fool all the people all the time." . . .

It cannot be denied that under this unhappy tendency to talk down to the Latin Americans there lurks a sense of superiority towards the "lesser breeds without the law" There are two Americas, and the Northern English-speaking, predominantly Protestant, gregarious, prosperous American looks down on the southern, Spanish- or Portuguese-speaking, Catholic, individualist, impecunious American not unlike the way Ulster looks down on Ireland. Underneath it all, the root cause of the trouble is the deep-lying anti-Spanish prejudice

in the American *ethos*. It betrays itself again in that very adjective
I have just used deliberately for the first time: *American*. The United
States of *America*. There is in this young, vigorous and healthy nation
a sense that the whole continent is its predestined estate, an impulse
(kept alive under more modern and genteel notions) which would
merely carry ever farther the expansion that turned the thirteen States
into the owner of the continent from the Atlantic to the Pacific and
from the Great Lakes to the Gulf. Now all this expansion, or most
of it, ran over lands of the Crown of Spain. It was hard for the
Northerner to suppress his feeling that the expansion of "America"
would know no other limits than those of America. Those Spaniards?
Well, what about them? What on earth are they there for, squatting
in our estate? This was not reason. It was life, manifest destiny.

Manifest destiny. The initials were the same as those of the Monroe
Doctrine. And when all is said and done, the Monroe Doctrine, by
its mere unilateralism, amounted to a degradation of the Latin American countries to the status of protectorates. Much water has flowed
over the rivers of both Americas since 1823, but the impulses and
attitudes which expressed themselves in the Monroe Doctrine remain
very much alive.

I remember that in the days when the spirited young men of the
State Department had not got to screen the fire of their eyes in order
not to dazzle the young men of the U.N. Secretariat, I was asked,
at question time at a banquet-cum-speech, what I thought of the
Monroe Doctrine. My answer was: "I only know two things about
the Monroe Doctrine: one is that no American I have met knows what
it is; the other is that no American I have met will consent to its
being tampered with. That being so, I conclude that the Monroe Doctrine is not a doctrine but a dogma, for such are the two features
by which you can tell a dogma. But when I look closer into it, I
find that it is not one dogma but two, to wit: the dogma of the infallibility of the American President and the dogma of the immaculate
conception of American foreign policy."

Years have gone by, and the American people have matured in matters of foreign policy with a speed unequalled elsewhere. And yet,
I suspect that though one hears less about the Monroe Doctrine than
in the days of old, the two dogmas have kept their vigorous hold
on the hearts of the people of the United States. There is in the Ameri-

can public a touching disposition to spontaneous acquiescence in what happens to be at the time the official line, a faith in the infallibility of the President and a staunch belief in the immaculate conception of the State Department's policy; both possibly animated by an even deeper degree of faith in the manifest destiny of the United States of America to become as big as her name. And it will be one of our tasks to try to find out how far this blustering spirit is still working under the internationally more respectable forms of Pan-american-led or other American-led institutions.

FRANCIS WILLIAMS
THE AMERICAN INVASION: DOLLARS ON THE MOVE

The American Invasion, *the subject of British author Francis Williams' book, is directed (if directed it is) from Wall Street rather than from Washington. His concern is with the implications of the growing American investments in Great Britain and other European countries in the decades after the Second World War. A more recent book on the same subject but with a title that suggests a rather different point of view is Jean-Jacques Servan-Schreiber's* The American Challenge *(1968). Recent developments in international economy, however, indicate that the era of American economic expansion in Europe may be over and that a counter trend of European capital entering the American market has begun. The following passages are taken from* The American Invasion *by Francis Williams (London: Anthony Blond, 1962), pp. 25-33. Copyright © 1962 by Francis Williams. Used by permission of Brown Publishers, Inc.*

Wherever there is a new and developing industry [in Britain] there American business has established a bridgehead.

We are still, of course, some distance away from the position of our oldest and closest relative in the Commonwealth, Canada. There more than fifty-two per cent of the entire industrial economy is now in American hands. The American grip on Canadian industry in fact has reached the stage where the freedom of the Canadian Government to take independent action in major spheres of economic policy in order to deal with unemployment and other important problems has, in the words of *The Times,* been 'substantially circumscribed'.

The intrusion of American capital here cannot in the nature of things reach the same scale as in Canadian economy. But it carries with it some of the same undertones of danger.

Consider, for example, one recent notorious issue which has roused Canadian public opinion to the dangerous position of subservience in which they find themselves.

The Canadian Government, like the British, recognizes mainland China. It encourages trade between the two countries in the interests both of international relations and Canada's economy. Recently a group of Canadian automobile companies with the strong encouragement of the Canadian Government, which was concerned about the level of unemployment in the industry, negotiated a contract for the sale of a substantial number of tractors to China. At once Detroit stepped in. Within a matter of hours the Canadian people were taught that the motor industry is one part of Canada in which the writ of the Canadian Government does not run.

Declaring the transaction to be contrary to *American* (although not Canadian) policy, American automobile manufacturers ordered all their Canadian affiliates to repudiate the contract without further notice. Apart from other considerations Canadian automobile workers were thus denied a sizeable and badly needed opportunity for employment in work favoured by their own Government at a time of mounting unemployment.

Two out of the four biggest motor manufacturers in Britain are now wholly American owned and controlled. Can we be sure that in similar circumstances they would be any more free from interference than the Canadian automobile manufacturers?

After the remarkable case of the six Viscounts the answer to such a question is no longer a matter of conjecture but fact. It is now quite clear that if occasion arises American control over vital elements of British industry will be used in exactly the same way and for exactly the same political purposes as in Canada.

Consider this Viscount case. In December 1961 it was announced that as part of a purely commercial transaction orders had been placed in Britain for six Viscount airliners for delivery to China. The planes concerned were civilian planes free of strategic embargo. The development of trade with mainland China—with which Britain, unlike America, has diplomatic and commercial relations—is an accepted British interest. The sale of the six Viscounts had therefore the full

approval of the British Government. It did not, however, find favour
in American eyes and on December 8th Mr. Dean Rusk the U.S. Secretary of State, made it known publicly that the American Government
disapproved of the transaction. This public statement was, according
to *The Times,* followed by an "unofficial" protest to the British
Government expressing the American Government's sharp disagreement with the approval given to the sale. The British Government
very sensibly ignored this protest. It repudiated the suggestion that
it should intervene against a perfectly proper commercial transaction
fully in line with official British policy. So far so good—or bad. Any
Government, of course, is perfectly entitled if it so wishes to express
its disagreement with another, although few, perhaps, are so apt as
American Governments to assume that they have the right to tell
friendly nations what they should or should not do.

What followed has a more sinister connotation—especially when
seen in the context of the immense expansion of American interests
in a number of key British industries already described. The British
company which is the main supplier of equipment for the instrument
landing system and V.O.R. navigational beacon receivers fitted in the
Viscount is the Standard Telephones and Cable Company. This equipment is recommended for world-wide navigational aids as a major contribution to air safety by the International Civil Aviation Organisation.
But Standard Telephones and Cables, which has total assets of over
£14,500,000 and is one of the biggest producers of telecommunications equipment in Britain, is wholly owned and controlled by the
International Telephone and Telegraph Company of New York and
governmental pressure having failed this economic power was now
invoked. In January it became known that the International Telephone
and Telegraph Company had been alerted and "cautioned" by the
U.S. State Department regarding the Viscount transaction, although
it had no direct concern with the supply of the equipment involved
none of which even was manufactured under American licence or
American patents: it had been designed in the British factory. Thereupon the International Telegraph and Telephone Company sent instructions to its British associate, Standard Telephones and Cables, warning
it that it must not provide equipment for any Viscounts intended for
China. By these means, to put it plainly, a deliberate attempt was

made to use American control of a British company to subvert British Government policy.

Fortunately in this instance it failed. Similar if not identical equipment was available from British companies not yet under American control. But who can say that as the American invasion proceeds similar pressure will not be employed in other industries in the future: or that a day will not come when it is effective—as it already has been in Canada. The sharp divergence of view between Britain and the United States on the recognition of mainland China is one of the facts of the international situation that has to be accepted. What ought not to be accepted, as the *Daily Telegraph* pointed out in its agreeably outspoken comments on the Viscount case, is that 'these differences should serve as a point of attack on an essentially commercial transaction . . . or that any pressure should be brought to bear on an American-owned company in this country to prevent the supply of air navigation equipment.' Yet this is exactly what happened.

The way in which American economic power was mobilised in this instance is even more relevant to an inquiry into the American invasion when the fact is taken into account that the field of telecommunications and precision instruments is one in which American infiltration has been particularly marked in recent years. Apart from Standard Telephones and Cables, itself, there are now in this and related fields at least nine British companies under American control. Many others are manufacturing under American licences. . . .

The industrial and political implications of the American invasion, which are already serious in Canada and potentially so in Britain, are not the only ones that have to be considered. To an extent exceeding any other in history American business is tied to the mass demand of a consumer market. It is significant that the largest concentration of American interests in British economy is in consumer trades whose success depends on persuading a British public to buy—and to some extent behave and think—like an American one.

Of course the total of British investment in American stocks and shares, although sadly depleted by the financial requirements of two wars, is also large. British investment helped to make the United States an industrial nation and it can be argued that what is happening now is that American investors are returning the compliment once paid to them by British investors. The two movements are not, however, comparable. British investment in America was commonly in capital industries. It helped American industry to build the railroads and make the machines that gave Americans what they wanted. It did not shape their wants. American investment in Britain on the other hand is predominantly in consumer and service industries. Such industries are directly tied to popular demand, or what can be made a popular demand by skilled promotion.

Moreover, to a much greater extent than was ever the case with British investment in American enterprises, what the Americans are buying is management control. American management, American ideas of what can be done to shape consumer demand, American methods in salesmanship and labour relations, move in along with American capital. What American business is seeking to export to Britain is not just money but American civilization and an American way of life. In an economy tied to a spiralling consumer demand this is the necessary noncomitant of success.

When Dr Dunning sent a questionnaire in 1956 to two hundred of the leading American financed firms in Britain he found that in 30 per cent of them half or more than half the Board was American and in 45 per cent more than a quarter. In the great majority of cases, moreover, all decisions of importance and their method of implementation had to be referred back for approval to the American parent company, including all changes in product range or design, advertising policy and the recruitment of senior staff.

This interference still operates at the top level. The Chairman of one of the largest American controlled firms in Britain with whom I was having dinner told me that his opposite number in the States was on the trans-Atlantic phone every day. 'But I had lunch yesterday with X' (Chairman of an even bigger one), he added. 'It was nice to know his chaps were even worse '

Dr Dunning found that on principle both American manufacturing techniques and managerial methods relating to production, purchasing, personnel, sales and advertising were assimilated and rigidly adhered to. A number of the British firms questioned commented that 'any new ideas or suggestions which it might put forward to its U.S. associate were squashed or treated with the greatest suspicion and rarely—if ever—acted upon'. Most of the American Managing Directors sent over when British firms were bought up or new subsidiaries launched were ex-sales executives and more American nationals were employed in the sales departments than in any other.

In one typical case where shortly after the war an important British company surrendered a 50 per cent interest in its equity capital to an American corporation, thirty-five key American executives were flown over within a matter of days to take command of all the important branches of the company's activities. British personnel are sent regularly each year to America for training.

In every case of American ownership expenditure on advertising and sales promotion has been sharply increased. The amount spent on advertising alone is three times as high as the share of total industrial output would call for in British terms and in a great many industries schools in American sales methods have been established not only for their own staffs but for those of their principal retail customers.

Nor is it only in British firms directly controlled from America that American methods are taking over. British management itself is steadily acquiring an American accent—even if it is sometimes a phoney one. The management consultants and efficiency experts, the men in the grey flannel suits, are moving deeper and deeper into British business life. Like their American counterparts businessmen here are learning that the unforgivable heresy is to think you know how to run your own business.

A Register of Management and Industrial Consultants was first established in Britain shortly after the end of the war on a model laid down by the Association of Consulting Management Engineers in the United States. At that time, although the Register was swollen by a number of accountancy firms which have since, for professional reasons, withdrawn, the total number of people engaged in management consultancy was just under 300. It is now, without the staffs of any firms of accountants, close on 1,300 and there are 28 firms engaged in the business, several of them with strong American affiliations. According to the Managing Director of one of the largest firms the new profession is now handling between 800 and 900 consultancy assignments and the number is steadily increasing. In September 1961 a Diploma in Management Studies was initiated. Sponsoring it, Sir David Eccles, whose taste in grey flannel suitings is of course impeccable, declared: 'We are still way behind the U.S. We must catch up.'

Along such trails as these—many of them no doubt admirable in themselves and capable of leading to richer living pastures—the American invasion makes its pervasive way. How pervasive one may discover if one visits one of those English towns which by some combination of circumstances have become peculiarly open to the impact of American ideas, in consequence, perhaps, of the decay of traditional industries and the development of new ones. Such towns represent a microcosm of a society in transition. In them old and new may be seen and compared side by side. Burnley, in Lancashire, is one of them.

Burnley was for generations a cotton town, living and working by, and for, one of the most traditional of British industrial processes. The houses clustered round the cotton mills in which not only the men but most of the women worked: a tough, idiosyncratic, humorous and independent people, lip-reading their ironic way through the noisy rattle of the looms in the damp air of the weaving sheds heavy with cotton fluff, and usually governed in their industrial affairs by what can best be described as an armed truce with the mill owners to whom they stood in a relationship more that of sub-contractors working a set of looms at their own pace than of employees called on to carry out a strictly disciplined task at speeds required of them by the management.

The conditions of the industry, rough and sometimes brutal yet conducive to independence, stamped the character of the town. It was a community in which everyone knew everyone else. The mill and the chapel were the centres of a society much more democratic in its attitudes than most in which men and women drew upon their own resources for happiness. Despite the ugliness of the back-to-back houses and the cobbled streets leading up to the bare hills the social life was energetic and outgoing. Within it the family was a tight, self-dependent unit.

Most of the cotton mills are closed now. Some have been made bankrupt by depression. In others the looms have been smashed and sold for scrap under a Government compensation scheme directed to bringing the cotton industry down to a size economically viable in current conditions. New industries have been brought in—bright, shining, modern industries making domestic equipment, radio parts, motor accessories, things of that sort. Several are American owned.

In the centre of the town a new skyscraper hotel rises above the mills—the first to be built outside London since the war. One walks through the wide doors into a lobby that might be that of an hotel in Chicago or Detroit. The bell-hop takes one up in the elevator to a room that with its sleek functionalism, its private bath, telephone and central heating, is a duplicate of thousands across the American continent. On the top floor there is an executive suite for the managing directors who fly in to see how their branch factories are doing. The dining-room has a chef from Monte Carlo and stays open until midnight. One looks out of the window expecting to find neon lights along Main Street: it comes as a shock to find they are not there yet. One feels suspended between two worlds.

In the town the cotton mills stand empty and derelict. The vast floor space of the weaving sheds echoes to the feet with the hollowness of the abandoned. They are no use to the new industries which require space for parking lots for the cars of the workers who come in from miles away in the American fashion. These new industries build on the periphery. Inside them everything is bright and clean. The damp humidity of the weaving sheds has been replaced by an air-conditioned purified atmosphere. Working to a schedule exactly contrived by the most scientific methods of time and motion study to secure the maximum output suited to their aptitude the women workers sit in bright, crisp nylon overalls doing the same thing over and over and over.

Transferred to this clinical perfection from their former jobs in the weaving sheds some of the women operators have been so ungrateful as to have nervous breakdowns. But the majority are happy in their work. It leaves them with unengaged minds. They can dream while their fingers follow their intricate but repetitive patterns. I asked one of them what she thought about. 'My boyfriend and going to America,' she said. And another. 'I think of my new hair-do and what's on the telly and why can't we have some of those drug stores they have in America?'

Outside the factory the parked cars give an American air to the scene. When the shift ends most of the cars turn outward away from the town. The old social life, born of the close community of home and mill and chapel, is shrinking. So far there is nothing much to replace it. 'If we are going to be an American town,' said one Councillor, 'then we shall have to have American amenities. Supermarkets, soda-fountains, late-night cinemas—the lot.'

An American town? Well, not quite. 'It's still sort of slow,' said the eager executive from Southern California who runs one of the American-owned plants. 'But you can feel things moving. The people are getting more like those back home. They're buying cars and going places. They shop around for jobs. They're more competitive and restless than they were. Yes, I think you could say they're getting Americanized . . .'

ALONSO AGUILAR
PAN-AMERICANISM

The United States has not always been a "good neighbor" to the Latin American countries. It is important that Americans try to appreciate how their country appears when viewed "from the other side," even though such an exercise in empathy may be difficult.

Alonso Aguilar is Professor of Economic Planning and Latin American Economic Development at the National University of Mexico. His Pan-Americanism from Monroe to the Present: A View from the Other Side *translated by Asa Zatz, was first published in 1965. The following excerpt is taken from pp. 155-165 of the New York edition of 1968 (Monthly Review Press). Copyright © 1968 by Monthly Review Press. Reprinted by permission of the copyright holder.*

For a hundred and fifty years Latin America has lived under the domination of foreign interests, its sovereignty alienated, and its principal sources of wealth in foreign hands. Monroeism, territorial expansion, manifest destiny, dollar diplomacy, Point Four, hemispheric solidarity, the struggle against international Communism, and the Alliance for Progress are not the expressions of fundamentally different policies but rather a series of names for the same old line of domination and plunder pursued on the continent to this day by the United States.

It would be difficult to evaluate precisely the amount of political, economic, and social damage that this subordination has brought the Latin-American countries, but it cannot be denied that it has been enormous and, in many cases, irreparable. Colonialism and imperialism have historically been the main obstacles to Latin-American development. During the century and a half of relative independence enjoyed by Latin America, the big Western powers, and the United States in particular, have smashed into its countries, violating them, deviating and arresting their development, irrationally exploiting their natural and human resources, subordinating entire nations to the mean and selfish interests of the big monopolies, more than once bathing their territories in the blood of criminal wars of conquest, mutilating their ancient cultures, and undermining the force of law to impose the law of force. Overpowering economic and diplomatic pressures have been brought to bear to support the outworn and backward in preserving their privileges, and to defend one freedom alone—that of free enterprise, trade, and exchange; in short, the freedom to exploit people and wealth with no restrictions whatsoever and with unbridled license.

For the people of Latin America, imperialism has meant subjugation, exploitation, constant meddling in their internal affairs, violations of sovereignty, irretrievable draining off of their nonrenewable natural resources to the point of exhaustion, extraction of economic surplus which under other historical conditions would have served to accelerate their own economic development, and violation of the right of self-determination of every nation—the right to choose the political and social system it prefers.

Imperialist policy during the last twenty years, far from changing to a form favorable to the economically backward nations of Latin America has, on the whole, become an increasingly aggressive and insurmountable obstacle to progress. The government of Franklin Roosevelt, as we have seen, opened new prospects for change and progress for the inter-American system. Even though the United States continued to defend its interests and often the interests of its great international monopolies, the struggle against Fascism and the danger of war, and the alliance with the Soviet Union during the war, encouraged the democratic forces of Latin America at certain moments—and, between 1933 and 1944, provided Pan-Americanism with its most favorable period. Since World War II, however, United States policy has become more and more irrational until it has culminated in the monstrous Johnson Doctrine which is, at bottom, an attempt to use the mechanism of "hemispheric solidarity" to counter the exercise of national sovereignty. According to that doctrine, the expansion of Communism in Europe or Asia, and the triumph of the Cuban Revolution, are no longer the only dangers to the continent; so is the determination of a people to overthrow a military dictatorship, as happened in Santo Domingo. And all this is in the interests of imperialism—interests which are audaciously and skillfully equated by their defenders with those of "Western civilization."

World War II not only rescued the Western World from the depression that followed the 1929 crash, but it also gave an enormous boost to the United States economy which, from that moment on, was to reach unprecedented levels of activity and win a dominant position in the so-called Free World, such as perhaps no power had ever had at any previous stage in history.

If the socio-economic conditions in the United States had changed in accordance with the policies of the New Deal during its best period and if the anti-monopoly struggle begun in the thirties had succeeded instead of having been given up, as was finally the case, surely the course of events since World War II would have been different. The monopolies, however, not only survived, but grew and consolidated themselves, broadening their field of action both outside and inside the country, and subjecting Latin America and other economically backward areas more profoundly to their domination. At the same time, even as peace was being restored, they successfully imposed the Cold War policy, and with it their thesis that the maintenance of an enormous military apparatus by the United States was the only means of insuring prosperity for its economy and that of the West in general. The adoption of a policy of huge military spending both internally and on the Cold War abroad, logically became two inseparable halves of the same policy.

It was not difficult to find a pretext for the adoption of this policy; Churchill and Truman found it in the expansion of socialism and the development of national liberation movements. A new phase in the process of historical development became converted, within the context of the narrow and reactionary ideology of subservience to imperialism, into a "sinister conspiracy," a "criminal subversive attempt," a "grave danger to Western civilization." . . .

The thesis that socialism, or simply the adoption of an advanced economic and social policy, involves grave threats to civilization and peace is an irrational, unscientific—truly incredible—concept which has nevertheless wormed its way into the ideology of Pan-Americanism and which has unscrupulously been put to use more and more frequently since the victory of the Cuban Revolution. But the people are beginning to understand much that escaped them before, to recognize that socialism is not incompatible with democracy, nor national liberation with Western civilization. What is actually incompatible with democracy is imperialism and all that its system implies in every one of the Latin-American countries: poverty, backwardness, dependence, and political regimes of force which regard the people as their most dangerous enemy.

Two decades ago, when Guatemala attempted to transform and modernize her weak and backward economy, to free herself from the oppressive yoke of the United Fruit Company and to stop being a "banana republic," she threatened no other country. She was not a danger to the peace of the world—not even to her closest neighbor, Mexico. When first President Quadros and then Goulart tried to initiate land reform in Brazil and to restrict the exportation of capital by foreign investors, they did not threaten any country either. The ones who denounced these acts as dangerous were Lacerda, then governor of the state of Guanabara, the most reactionary Brazilian landowners, and the United States government—all of whom soon showed their hands when they publicly congratulated the military officers who carried out the *coup* that ended constitutional government. When the Cuban people overthrew Batista, when the revolutionary government decreed the nationalization of large United States enterprises, and when Fidel Castro said he was a Marxist-Leninist—in none of these cases was the peace or security of the continent endangered, though it was understandable how keenly the foreign interests which had had Cuba in their hands for more than half a century felt the threat to their hegemony in Latin America.

The recent course of Pan-Americanism, in large measure an expression of the imperialist trend of policy in Latin America, is disquieting. The phase in which possible military attack by an extra-continental power could automatically involve the nations in a military conflict alien to their interests has been superseded by resolutions which have been accepted weakly and without dignity by their foreign ministers under pressure from the United States. The thesis of the "incompatibility of totalitarianism" and "representative democracy" brought to Bogotá by General Marshall as one of the first contributions of Cold War policy to those countries, has since developed significantly. What was really incompatible as far as the OAS was concerned was not totalitarianism but the Guatemala of Arévalo and Arbenz and the Cuba of Fidel Castro. They were incompatible despite the fact that both countries represented two of the most genuine examples of democracy America has known in recent times. Incompatible with the OAS were, in fact, the progressive reforms which Brazil tried to carry out under the government of Goulart and the struggle of the Dominican people to re-establish and enforce the Constitution and the democratic freedom it guaranteed. Incompatible with the interests of the United States government and the monopolies was the democratic revolution in Bolivia as expressed in Paz Estenssoro. Both the repudiation of totalitarianism and the defense of true representative democracy are so far from really being the concern of the OAS that not a single one of its members requested the convocation of a consultative meeting to study the danger to the continent represented by the "gorillarchies"; not one of them has denounced the governments of Nicaragua or Guatemala, Venezuela or Columbia, or the dictatorial regimes in Ecuador, Brazil, and Paraguay; not one has requested that the OAS, in accordance with its Charter, put an end to the criminal violations by the United States in Santo Domingo.

The countries of America face a dilemma: either they resign themselves to living in poverty and backwardness, dependent upon other countries, working without hope and standing by as their wealth is siphoned off for the benefit of others, or they decide to stand up, live with dignity, demand respect for their rights, and courageously confront the obstacles impeding and deforming their development.

Economic development is not only a question of investments or of the use of new techniques; it is a process which presupposes profound changes, blocked so far in Latin America by imperialism and the oligarchies serving it. If the Latin-American countries are to industrialize rapidly and raise the living standards of their people, they will have to carry out structural changes which release productive forces, accelerate the capital-formation process, expand foreign markets, mobilize and activate their creative energies, and modify their foreign-relations framework to make possible a fair and balanced type of trade which will in turn foster speedy and independent development.

Structural changes are not easily made, however, since they inevitably affect the interests of national sectors and foreign investors who obtain multiple benefits from the existing situation. It would be naive, at this point, to think that the United States and the privileged groups in the Latin-American countries oppose only Communist movements. Mexico's experience in its revolutionary stage and that of Guatemala, Brazil, Cuba, and particularly Santo Domingo, show that such is not the case and that the margin for peaceful social and political change is constantly narrowing.

This question is so important that it is worth stressing. Any progressive national program that affects the interests of the monopolies, or of the national bourgeoisie linked to them; any real advance in land reform; any more or less serious attempt at planning which reduces the radius of action of "free enterprise" and imperialism, which tends to replace anarchy with a minimum measure of rationality, or which impinges on vested interests in one way or another; any structural change, in fact, which oversteps the innocuous and ineffectual limits of the Alliance for Progress, will be stubbornly and even violently obstructed by national and foreign ruling groups, by the social and political forces which fear progress and know that their privileges will never be safe in a dynamic community determined to eliminate the factors producing backwardness.

It would be simple to renounce such changes and seek an easier and bloodless path which might reconcile clashing interests and avoid social conflicts and tensions. But it is only the superficial schemes of reformists like Teodoro Moscoso or Luis Muñoz Marín which are constructed around this possibility.

Changes are imperative and many of them can no longer be delayed. Latin America will be unable to achieve any progress worthy of the name unless it institutes a different agrarian structure; another system of distribution which liberates small producers from speculation and parasitism; an effective nationalist policy to rescue the lands, mines, industries, transportation, banks, and in general, the means of production still in foreign hands; a bold anti-monopoly policy; open and growing trade with all countries, particularly the socialist group; an independent labor and peasant movement; and at least a minimum of rational economic planning and true political democracy.

What makes Latin America's situation more difficult and pressing is that it is not only just such essential reforms and changes that the government of the United States, the ministers of the OAS and, particularly, the Johnson Doctrine consider "incompatible with representative democracy" but even the very historical process toward higher and more rational forms of organization of economic and social life. . . .

The idea is frequently advanced that, given their present status, Latin-American countries have no choice but to withdraw from the OAS. The problem is more complex and difficult than that. It is evident that the OAS has become an instrument of United States imperialism. The actual instruments, however, are the governments which increasingly divorce themselves from their people and go to Washington to pay tribute to their master and to receive instructions on how to act at the first sign of popular unrest.

Latin America must choose the road it is going to follow from now on, and this can be done inside or outside the OAS, as it can be done inside or outside the UN. The thing that is really important to understand is that the Pan-Americanism of Johnson and the OAS is by no means the culmination of what Bolívar envisioned before the Congress of Panama 150 years ago, but quite the opposite; and that imperialism is not defending Western or any other civilization, but only its own interests and its own hegemony which are indeed in danger in countries where the people have launched themselves on the conquest of their liberation.

To defend freedom and justice is one thing, but to support anarchy and privilege is something quite different. Freedom for the monopolies engenders the servitude and backwardness of peoples. To set up Anglo-Saxon democracy as the model for all nations to copy, when such a model was never realized in Europe even during the competitive phase of capitalist development, is to put progress in a strait jacket and, what is even more unacceptable, to seek to condition the exercise of sovereignty and the right of self-determination to suit the interests of a few big imperialist powers.

Democracy cannot be pressed into a static and inflexible mold. Anglo-Saxon or otherwise. The form that the political regime of any nation takes must be the fruit of its special conditions and traditions, of the development of its society, and the free choice of its people. The zeal of the OAS and the State Department in seeking to impose a supposed form of democracy as the only true, legal, and viable one is indeed touching; it demonstrates the irrationality with which Pan-Americanism has been seized since the anti-Communist Rio Treaty and, most of all, under the Johnson Doctrine. And if such a stereotype of democracy seems unacceptable, it is positively grotesque to confuse it with that rare species of "representative democracy" which is being forced upon Latin America at all costs; a "democracy" without the people and against the people which in reality represents only privileged and decadent minorities, reactionary military castes, illegally enriched officialdom, foreign businessmen of all sorts, to say nothing of a swarm of scabs, informers, witch hunters, secret police, FBI and CIA agents, and other "forces" upon which many "representative democracies" are based today and which the Alliance for Progress vainly tries to whitewash.

G. A. ARBATOV
AMERICAN IMPERIALISM AND NEW WORLD REALITIES

While one may feel that the Latin American contributors to this volume are justified in the harshness of their criticism of United States foreign policy, it may be more difficult to accept a self-righteous criticism from someone speaking for another super power. For while liberals and conservative humanists may be extremely critical of the United States, socialists, on the other hand, have not always had reason to be happy with the policy of the Soviet Union, domestic or foreign. Nevertheless, G. A. Arbatov, who is director of the U.S.S.R. Academy of Sciences's Institute on the U.S.A., is a close student of American politics and his Marxist analysis is also an indication of the changing attitudes in the Soviet Union to the United States. Excerpts from his article on "American Imperialism and New World Realities," which first appeared in Pravda *on May 4, 1971, is taken from the translation in* The Current Digest of the Soviet Press, *XXIII, no. 18 (June 1,*

1971), pp. 1-3, 8. Translation copyright 1974 by The Current Digest of The Soviet Press, *published weekly by the American Association for the Advancement of Slavic Studies; reprinted by permission of the Digest.*

The past five-year period can rightly be considered a very critical period in the history of American imperialism. Social and political contradictions in the United States have taken on the nature of an acute crisis. . . .

In the 1965-1970 period the U.S.A. was characterized not only by mounting internal difficulties and problems but also by the increasingly organic interlacing of those difficulties with foreign-policy problems. Above all, this involves the war in Southeast Asia, which has already become the most protracted and one of the bloodiest and most expensive wars the U.S.A. has waged in its entire history. Dissatisfaction with the war in Vietnam has created a situation in which many hundreds of thousands of Americans have taken a new look at the arms race, at the influence that militarist circles and the military-industrial complex have acquired in the country, and at the entire policy of American imperialism, which lays claim to the mission of world gendarme. . . .

The connection between the Vietnam war, the unchecked arms race and the whole imperialist course of U.S. policy on the one hand and the aggravation of domestic problems on the other has become an indisputable fact today for a significant part of the American public. In some cases, this connection is direct—the fact that young people do not want to sacrifice their lives in a war that they consider immoral and criminal plays a considerable role in students' antigovernment actions. In other cases, an indirect influence is involved, an influence connected, for example, with the fact that military expenditures limit even more the already meager appropriations for solving many domestic social problems and spur inflation. . . . But millions of Americans are losing the blind faith that has been instilled in them for so long that capitalist America and its policy are supposedly the highest achievement of world civilization and that this gives Washington the right to remake the world in accordance with its own image and likeness. Broad dissatisfaction, disillusionment and deepening political polarization have worked to change this belief.

The change in the country's moral and political climate has affected not only the broad public but also the ruling circles. Growing uneasiness, doubt with respect to the correctness of the policy that is being pursued and anxiety concerning the fact that the U.S.A. is entering a period of profound and dangerous internal convulsions became characteristic of significant numbers of them during these years.

II.—The past five-year period confronted imperialism, including American imperialism, with new realities—above all a further change in the alignment of forces between the two world social and economic systems in favor of socialism. Throughout the past few years, this process has grown in two ways, so to speak. It has proceeded both through the further strengthening of the positions of the Soviet Union, the other socialist countries and the international workers' and liberation movements and through the serious exacerbation of the internal contradictions in the imperialist camp itself. . . .

The C.P.S.U. Central Committee's Report to the 24th Party Congress notes the bourgeoisie's endeavor to employ more camouflaged forms of the exploitation and oppression of the working people and its readiness in a number of cases to undertake partial reforms in order to keep the masses under its ideological and political control as much as possible. The monopolies' attempts to use the achievements of scientific and technical progress for strengthening their own positions, for increasing the efficiency and development rates of production and for intensifying the exploitation of the working people and their oppression have received wide dissemination.

The foreign policy of imperialism is also marked by attempts to adapt to new world realities. Thus, new and more refined forms of neocolonialism are replacing the traditional forms of colonial oppression. In addition to the old methods of combating socialism, some new methods are being put into practice. In their foreign and domestic policy, the imperialist powers are sometimes compelled to make partial concessions in order to forestall still greater shocks.

American policy's first major confrontation with the new realities of the postwar world took place back in the late 1950s and early 1960s. At that time it became clear, among other things, that U.S. imperialism's reliance on military might as its main weapon in the struggle against the Soviet Union and the other socialist countries had been checkmated as a result of the changing alignment of military forces. By the late 1950s, the U.S.S.R.'s economic, scientific, technical and social successes had made it necessary to answer socialism's "peaceful challenge," which was becoming especially impressive against the background of the instability and disorder in the American economy and the serious internal difficulties in the U.S.A.

At that time, a sharp debate developed in the country around the fundamental problems of American policy. Roughly speaking, the struggle was waged around the question: Should the policy be changed, should we reach some new adaptation of policy to new conditions? President J. Kennedy, in the last period of his administration, began to speak out in favor of taking the new alignment of forces in the world into consideration, of not relying exclusively on nuclear weapons, and of trying to solve—even if only partially—the U.S.A's most critical domestic problems. Such views exacerbated the struggle in the ruling circles of the U.S.A. This became evident in the 1964 presidential election, in which L. Johnson came out with a platform that claimed to be a continuation of Kennedy's policies, while Goldwater, with his "conservative" program, personified the most reactionary and aggressive circles of the American bourgeoisie. This struggle, as is known, ended with Goldwater's defeat.

The following years have emphasized with special force the discrepancy between U.S. foreign policy and the contemporary world situation. It does not follow from this that the struggle in the ruling class has ended—today it is being waged with perhaps even greater acerbity. But to a large extent it is now being waged around a different question: Just how should we adapt? Here two directions have been revealed quite distinctly.

One of them is the adaptation primarily of methods and forms, which envisages searches for more subtle and more cunning methods of implementing the same reactionary domestic policy and the same foreign policy course, which is aimed at maintaining international tension and at continuing military adventures.

The other direction, along with improving the former policy methods, envisages a certain correction in policy itself and consideration for the realities of the present-day world, not only in terms of form, but also in terms of essence (needless to say, only to a certain extent, limited by the class interests of the bourgeoisie).

As the experience of the past few years shows, the first of the directions mentioned above has become more characteristic of the U.S.A. For example, if we were to analyze the domestic political activity of the American government during the past few years, we would see that far greater attention is devoted to questions of political methods (improving the administrative apparatus, seeking more efficient means of combating the opposition, and also more skillfully combining ideological influence on broad strata of the public with repressions against the most active fighters against oppression and injustice, etc.) than to substantive solutions to the most crucial domestic problems.

Perhaps this relates to foreign policy to an even greater extent. Although all the experience of past years bespeaks the futility of trying to attain its foreign-policy goals with the help of military force, the U.S. government has directed its principal efforts not at resolving disputed questions with the help of negotiations but at improving its military machine and at seeking ways for broadening its "applicability" (through the utilization and strengthening of the military potential of its allies, as envisaged by the "Nixon Doctrine," the introduction of new types of weapons and tactics, etc.) Although the whole experience of the war in Vietnam indicates its complete hopelessness for the U.S.A., Washington, instead of ending this disgraceful war, is directing its principal efforts at something completely different—at searching for methods to muffle the opposition within the U.S.A., thereby providing itself with the opportunity of continuing the aggression for an indeterminate period.

The same also applies to U.S. policy in the Near East, its position on the question of the strategic arms race and its relations with the Soviet Union, in which the slogan about "the transition from an era of confrontation to an era of negotiation" has become essentially a means of soothing the public, not a realistic program for normalizing relations and improving the international situation.

Can such a line, the endeavor to reduce adaptation to the new world situation merely to the modernization of methods and means, bring any substantial results in solving the problems that the United States is running into? The concrete facts of political life give a negative answer to this question. . . .

III.—Naturally, the question arises: How should the attempts of the imperialist bourgeoisie to adapt to the new world situation be treated?

This question has not only theoretical interest—it is also important for working out a correct policy and tactics for the anti-imperialistic struggle.

The answer to this question cannot be a simple one. It depends above all on exactly what kind of adaptation one is talking about in each concrete case—about the steps aimed at deceiving the working people and misleading the public, about more refined attempts to attain the same aggressive, imperialistic goals, or about practical changes in policy that take the realities of today's world into account.

In the first case, the unmasking of the maneuvers of imperialism and the frustration of these maneuvers is the only possible answer.

As far as imperialism's attempts to make realistic corrections in its policy are concerned, this is a more complex matter.

In this case also, a class approach to the problem demands a clear understanding of the fact that no matter how far the process of the adaptation of imperialism to the situation goes, this does not change the nature of imperialism or the oppressive essence of this system. This distinguishes the Marxist-Leninist approach from the reformist and revisionist approach, which essentially preaches the accommodation of the workers' movement to present day imperialism and a reconciliation with it.

But it does not at all follow from this that elements of realism in the domestic and foreign policies of the capitalist powers have no importance and should be rejected on the ground that such attempts express an endeavor to preserve imperialism, to prevent new shocks and political failures for imperialism. Needless to say, any concessions by imperialism, any steps in the direction of adapting to the existing situation, objectively express this kind of class interest of the bourgeoisie. But such steps signify forced concessions under the pressure of the forces of peace and progress and objectively can have consequences that correspond to the peoples' interests. What we are talking about here is not only a matter of economic concessions that are extracted by the working people in the course of intense class struggle.

The working class in the capitalist countries is by no means indifferent to whether it lives in conditions of a terrorist dictatorship of the fascist type or in conditions of bourgeois democracy. In exactly the same way, people, including the peoples of socialist states, are by no means indifferent to the direction in which international relations develop—in the direction of preparations for thermonuclear war or in the direction of the peaceful coexistence of states and a political detente, which, of course, does not abolish the struggle between the two systems itself but moves it into channels in which this struggle does not lead to military conflict. The significance of these distinctions was emphasized by V. I. Lenin, who pointed out that one should take different attitudes toward those representatives of the bourgeois camp who "gravitate toward the military resolution of questions" and toward those who "gravitate toward pacifism, even if they are of the very worst sort and, from the standpoint of communism, cannot withstand even the slightest criticism."

The 24th Party Congress demonstrated once again that our party is firmly pursuing Leninist principles in foreign policy. The comprehensive program of peace put forward by the Congress is addressed not only to the masses of working people in all countries but to the bourgeois governments, to those representatives of the bourgeoisie that see the necessity of bringing the policy of these governments into line with the demands and realities of the present-day situation.

This also applies to the line formulated by the Congress on the question of Soviet-American relations, which combines a readiness to normalize these relations and to resolve disputed questions by means of negotiation with a firm rebuff to the aggressive impulses of American imperialism with respect to the U.S.S.R. or any other country or people in the world.

The future will show the direction that the further evolution of American policy will take. One thing is clear: No maneuvers and no attempts to reduce the matter to the modernization of the methods and means of imperialist policy without making practical, realistic corrections in it will open up prospects for normalizing the international situation. They do not open up any kind of acceptable prospects for the American people themselves or for the true national interests of America.

VII. EPILOGUE: THREAT OR PROMISE

How much is left in the 1970s of the kind of hope the John Stracheys of Europe had in America in the 1930s? At times it may seem that the staunchest friends and supporters of America abroad are the many right-wing totalitarian regimes in Europe, Latin America and Asia that rely on United States support. That the two national leaders who seemed to enjoy each others company most in 1973 were Soviet Party Leader Leonid Brezhnev and U.S. President Richard Nixon did not necessarily make the outlook brighter for those who hope for a future where the world is not entirely controlled by two or three super powers. Why is it so easy for Washington to communicate with Peking and yet it was impossible to have had friendly relations with Santiago, which, under Allende, had one of the most significant democratic, social experiments in the world today? Such questions may reflect the outlook of a citizen of a small country, but it is, again, a point of view that Americans should try to appreciate.

All over the world people are concerned about the direction American society is taking because they know it will effect their own lives. The two persons who have been selected to conclude this volume have both reflected on the potential of America on the basis of an intimate knowledge of this country. But there similarity ends. Jean-François Revel's *Without Marx or Jesus* sees America in the process of revolutionary change; Johan Galtung sees the country heading toward disaster.

What are the surface symptoms of anti-Americanism in the world today? What are the underlying causes? Is the amount or the virulence of anti-Americanism justified, according to Revel? What hope does

America offer that it can correct itself in the near future? What indications exist that it cannot?

JEAN-FRANCOIS REVEL
ANTI-AMERICANISM AND THE AMERICAN REVOLUTION

Jean-François Revel's Without Marx or Jesus: The New American Revolution Has Begun *(1971) is perhaps the most provocative of recent studies of the United States. His thesis is summed up in the concluding paragraph: "Today in America—the child of European imperialism—a new revolution is rising. It is* the revolution of our time. *It is the only revolution that involves radical, moral, and practical opposition to the spirit of nationalism. It is the only revolution that, to that opposition, joins culture, economic and technological power, and a total affirmation of liberty for all in place of archaic prohibitions. It therefore offers the only possible escape for mankind today: the acceptance of technological civilization as a means and not as an end, and—since we cannot be saved either by the destruction of the civilization or by its continuation—the development of the ability to reshape that civilization without annihilating it." Revel's optimism is not shared by many other observers of the American scene, natives nor foreigners, but his critique of some of the excesses of "anti-Americanism" deserve to be considered carefully, not the least by Americans who often seem the most one-sided critics of their own country.*

The following pages are taken from "Anti-Americanism and the American Revolution" which appears in the book Without Marx or Jesus: The New American Revolution Has Begun *by Jean-François Revel. Translated by Jack Bernard. Translation copyright © 1971 by Doubleday & Company, Inc. Used by permission of the publisher.*

Anti-Americanism is one of the great psychological phenomena of our time. Moreover, it is a phenomenon that must be taken into account in that mixture of fact and hypothesis which allows us to conclude that America faces a future of revolution, and that the American Revolution will be the one most likely to bring about the changes that the modern world needs.

It is difficult to determine the causes of anti-Americanism without describing its symptoms. The two factors are inseparable, even though the symptoms are amenable to analysis, while the causes are only a matter of conjecture. In analyzing the symptoms, we must distinguish two basic kinds of anti-Americanism. There is one kind, which is founded· on reasonable criticism and on precise data, and which is justifiable in relation to political goals and clear value judgments. And there is another kind of anti-Americanism, characterized by a quality of obsession, and by the rejection of any attempt at rational appraisal—or even irrational, but intelligible, appraisal. By an "irrational, but intelligible, appraisal" I mean a point of view which, even though it may be partisan and subjective, may still be modified by a presentation of facts. For there are partisan positions that have a form; and there are partisan positions that have no form. In the first case, whether we are talking about arguments or about sympathies and antipathies, there are clearly distinguishable pros and cons. In the second case, the pros and cons frequently exchange places, because they are based only on emotion, which itself is changeable; and so, with arguments for and against something being used interchangeably, the only consistent element is the person's determination to preserve his grievances intact.

Let me give an example of what I mean. Early in 1970, I visited the United States for a few weeks. (That was not a long time—but it was long enough to make me forget, or at least to make me less conscious, of some of the absurd themes so familiar in Europe.) Upon my return to France, I was astonished by some of the responses to my comments on America. I said, for instance, that the United States seemed to be in the process of change; that protest, dissent, and opposition to authority and to the past seemed more pronounced there than anywhere else. The answer I got was: "The assassination of Martin Luther King, and the trial of James Earl Ray, prove, beyond the slightest doubt, that America is a fascist power."

This kind of answer has several causes. First of all, it did not contradict what I had just said (even though it was intended to do so) because political assassinations and dubious trials are hardly incompatible with a revolutionary situation. Quite the contrary. It springs, I think, from an unwillingness to use facts as the basis of opinions, or to regard certain kinds of facts even as remotely possible. It also reflects a determination to regard, as specifically American, certain situations that, in fact, are less serious in America than elsewhere. There is something wrong when we hear the whole of America condemned on the basis of a single questionable trial—especially when that condemnation takes place in the country of the Ben Barka affair; or when we hear America condemned for violence, in a country where the O.A.S. flourished. One wonders what a French leftist would say if we put Pompidou's words into his mouth, and then criticized him for it? What would be the reaction of an Italian communist if we tried to prove that Italy is fascist by citing the position of a socialist leader? The Frenchman would answer that the May uprisings and M. Pompidou are two different things. And the Italian would answer that, after all, not all Italians belong to the Socialist Party. Yet, in the case of America, we are unwilling to make the same distinctions. The European Left refuses to admit even that there is an American Left —let alone that it is more powerful than the European Left. We seem to be incapable of recognizing anything but Rightist tendencies. And that inability makes it possible for one of France's most intelligent and sophisticated political commentators to say: "In the United States, Mr. Nixon's only serious rival, for the moment, is the racist Wallace."

On the whole, American dissent has had much better luck than the European counterpart in attaining well-defined goals. Once again (because it is important), I cite, as an example, the research centers that have refused to undertake, or to continue, projects of military value. On the other hand, university dissent in America did not succeed, as it did in Europe, in completely closing down the schools. But then, American higher education has not been weakened either by change or by its inability to change. The approximately twenty thousand students at Berkeley continue to receive an education that is regarded as the finest available in America—and probably in the world; and this in spite of the fact that the Sorbonne-like immensity of the institution and of the plant causes problems similar to those of European universities. In other words, American dissent has been able to avoid one of the great dangers of change: the destruction of the object of change before change can be affected, in which case the revolution leads to underdevelopment and, thereby, destroys itself.

American dissent therefore fulfills (despite some of its negative aspects) one of the necessary conditions for revolution: it is contesting moral values, modifying alternatives, and, in general, criticizing cultural standards. Moreover—and this is very important—dissent is doing all this within the context of the American situation as a whole. And, in any event, its effectiveness is undeniable, and superior to that of dissent in France.

One day, I told a Frenchman about American student participation in the California grape strike. For a second, it looked as though he were going to be deprived of his image of America as reactionary. But then he came up with an answer. "Nonsense," he said, "they're probably eating grapes from Israel." The utter absurdity of exporting grapes from Israel to California never occurred to him, let alone the fact that having Israeli grapes available in California would have put the California grape growers in a worse predicament than ever. What he was concerned about was identifying his two pet hates: Yankee capitalism, and Zionist imperialism—the latter being a disguise of the former. Following that line of thought, it became clear that the students were supporting the Chicanos in order (somehow) to enslave the Palestinian Arabs. And the logical circle was complete. I should point out one thing: the man I was talking to was not some drunk I met in a bar, or an uniformed Maoist crank, but a well-known political journalist—a man who is thought of as a "great reporter."

According to this man's thinking, the imperialistic pro-Zionism of the United States does not prevent Americans from being rabidly anti-Semitic at home. And this anti-Semitism is but one aspect of the overall racism which is, as every good European knows, the chief characteristic of Americans. In fact, shortly after leaving my great-reporter friend, I ran into a lady novelist of the extreme Left, who asked me, in a tone that implied she already knew the answer, whether there was "still as much anti-Semitism in America." I answered that I had always heard that there was a certain amount of anti-Semitic discrimination in America, in certain clubs and restaurants, but that I had never seen any during my visits there. She counterattacked vigorously, offering to show me a list of some twenty or thirty New York restaurants where people with Jewish names were automatically refused reservations. To avoid a fight, I answered that her information might be correct, but that it did not coincide with my own impressions of America. And I added: "Moreover, there is a law in New York against discrimination in public places. If anyone does discriminate, he can be taken to court." And there the discussion ended. It was not until I had a chance to think about what the lady said that I reached the boiling point. There are presently six million Jews in America. Why are they there? Because they, or their parents or grandparents, were chased out of Europe by persecutions, or by pogroms at the beginning of the century in Russia, and in Hungary, Romania, and Poland. They are in America because in Europe we had Hitler, and the racial laws of Vichy France, and roundups of Jews in France. In fact, at the very moment that that woman was lecturing me on anti-Semitism in America, there were signs of a strange public delirium in France, in the form of rumors: a "rumor from Orléans," a "rumor from Amiens." The content of these rumors was that women in those two cities had gone into Jewish stores—and had never been heard from again.

Barbarous, bloody, fanatic, narrow, repressive Europe. Europe, which has always practiced anti-Semitism in all its forms, from subtle harassment to planned genocide; Europe, which climbed to the pinnacle of anti-Semitism in our own time, and, during the Second World War, killed almost twice as many Jews as are presently living in the United States. And I had listened politely to a European, a Frenchwoman, as she condemned American anti-Semitism in the allocation of reservations in a restaurant.

Not long after that encounter, I went to see a documentary film of Frédéric Rossif's, entitled *Pourquoi l'Amérique?* (Why America?). If one can take the film at face value, the whole history of the United States between the world wars is the story of Prohibition and its effects, the judicial crime of which Sacco and Vanzetti were the victims, the clubbing of workers by the police, and the F.B.I. Only the most absurd comments by American public officials were included in the film; and they were described as stupid by the commentary, and greeted by loud laughter from the audience. Roosevelt's social reforms were mentioned, of course, but no one was allowed to understand how they came about, because nothing was mentioned about the leftist principles of Roosevelt's advisers. Nor was anything said about the state of public opinion which allowed Roosevelt easily to be re-elected three times. Indeed, it was impossible to believe that he could have been elected even once, since the country described in *Pourquoi l'Amérique?* was populated almost exclusively by lynch-crazed mobs of racists, brutal policemen, grotesque society ladies, and gangsters. In the sequence concerning the beginning of the war in 1939, the main emphasis was on one of Charles Lindbergh's pro-Hitler speeches, to the position of the extreme Right-wingers, and to the American Nazi Party. On the basis of history as presented by M. Rossif, it is hard to understand how the United States ended up arming and equipping the British and the Russians, as well as its own men, between 1942 and 1944. And it is impossible to understand how this crime-ridden and idiotic nation, after having intervened directly in Europe and assured the victory of the Allies, could have emerged from the war as the greatest economic, political, technological, and scientific power of the world. A strange destiny for a nation composed of brutes and fascists.

It may be that Europeans are right about America. If so, I am unable to explain why Europe, and not America, has been blessed with Hitler, Mussolini, the Moscow Trials, concentration camps, Pétainism, Franco-ism, racial persecution, the Gestapo, the G.P.U., and the political hatreds of Germany, Soviet Russia, Spain, France, and Italy. Why is it that the United States has always been able to preserve its democratic institutions and avoid fascism? And why is it that totalitarian regimes occupy the major part of European history in the twentieth century, and most of European territory today? In other words, we are being asked to believe that the causes of fascism have always existed in America, and that they are becoming more pronounced today; but, by some mysterious process, fascism itself always appears in Europe, and never in America. It is a paradox, of course; but we have gotten too accustomed to it to realize it. Even the political analysts do not seem puzzled by the fact that the seed of fascism is always sown in America—and always becomes a tree in Europe. Ever since I was old enough to tell the difference between Europe and America on the map, I have heard predictions of the growth of the fascist Right in America, and of the socialist Left in Europe. If those forecasts are correct, we are confronted by one of the great mysteries of contemporary history. We will never be able to understand why, in the last fifty years, so many millions of Europeans have fled to America to escape persecution, and so few Americans have fled to Europe. . . .

Sometimes the purpose of anti-Americanism is to shore up our own sense of intellectual and moral superiority. And sometimes it indicates an unwillingness to take into account any fact that might disturb our prejudices. In the latter case, we are capable of extraordinary subtlety in coming up with unfavorable interpretations of any experience. Under this heading we can group our "proofs" of the inferiority of American culture. One day I told a friend of mine that, during a visit to the United States, I had met some very intelligent people and, above all, many different kinds of people. (That was the worst thing I could have said. Everyone knows that all Americans are imbeciles and conformists.) In rebuttal, my friend told me about an evening he had spent in California, during which he had not heard a single human voice. The only audible sounds were those of washing machines, vacuum cleaners, and lawn mowers. Even if my friend could prove to me that evenings in Castlenaudary or Pont-à-Mousson are spent discussing the *Parmenides*, I would still not believe that his California example has a statistical value. For him, the memory of California has another value: it is a place of refuge, where he is protected from the humiliation of having to admit the possibility of a cultivated America.

A favorite target of anti-Americanism is the American politician, who is uniformly presented as a prodigy of bland self-conceit. Into this category are thrown both wheat and chaff, without distinction. There is Truman, "the haberdasher," belching out vulgarisms; and "smiling Ike," absorbed in his game of golf. In Rossif's film, *Pourquoi l'Amérique?*, one of the biggest laughs of the evening came when President Hoover was shown speaking his famous sentence: "We stand at the threshold of an era of prosperity without precedent in the history of the world"—words spoken only a few weeks before the crash of 1929. It was an unhappy choice of words, given what was immediately to follow—but neither inaccurate nor ridiculous, given what was to come ten or fifteen years later. Immediately after the Second World War the United States entered the age of mass consumption and attained a standard of living "without precedent in the history of the world." (Whether or not one likes the *kind* of life that that standard entails, is another question.) Political prophecies that are fulfilled are a great rarity; let alone political prophecies that are fulfilled in fifteen years. Therefore, Hoover's words, as disastrous as they seemed at the time, are much less so in retrospect. . . .

In the light of all this, one can understand why Jean-Jacques Servan-Schreiber's *American Challenge* aroused such fury in European "progressivist" circles. The book's thesis was that American successes were due more to intelligence than to force or to the abundance of natural resources. It was an intolerable opinion, but a strangely attractive one. And it stirred up a burning indignation—but indignation that was, at the same time, ambiguous and contradictory. That is in the nature of things; for we cannot deliberately ignore something real unless we are aware that it exists.

The most humiliating kind of defeat is a cultural defeat. It is the only defeat that one can never forget, because it cannot be blamed on bad luck, or on the barbarism of the enemy. It entails not only acknowledgment of one's own weakness, but also the humiliation of having to save oneself by taking lessons from the conqueror—whom one must simultaneously hate and imitate. It was for that reason that *The American Challenge* was virtuously denounced and, at the same time, avidly read. And this brings us to the second part of the anti-American phenomenon: a systematically unfavorable interpretation of everything American, to which is added the painful knowledge that this interpretation is worthless. When our backs are against the wall, we admit that American successes may not be pure luck, and that they may be due to the importance which both the government and private enterprise attach to basic research. But then we save face by poking fun at "American management," and by declaring that, since we reject American goals, we can hardly be jealous of American methods. In other words, the news that America has accomplished something is the signal for us to say that that accomplishment is worthless. When the American work week is shortened through automation, we say that Americans are technological slaves. When they reduce poverty, we sniff and talk about the "consumer society." And yet, the latter accomplishments are two of the secular goals of utopic or "scientific" socialism.

We might ask ourselves if anti-Americanism, while apparently directed against the Rightist aspects of American society, is not sometimes inspired instead by a fear of the upheavals in America—i.e., a fear that they may spread to the rest of the world. And that fear, in the final analysis, is really a fear of revolution. If that is not so, how can we explain the fact that a man in 1970 can persist in believing, all evidence to the contrary, that America is inhabited not only by conservatives, but, like all other countries, by opposing groups? How can he ignore the evidence that a battle is being fought in the United States, that its outcome is uncertain, but that the stakes are of the utmost importance for all mankind? Why would he breathe a sigh of relief every time he has the opportunity to strengthen his belief that reaction is triumphant in the United States?

If Anti-Americanism is indeed founded on fear of revolution, it may be that the anti-Americanism of the Left is not very different from that of the Right. They are both dictated by a fear of change, and by a feeling of resentment at the thought that a civilization other than their own has come to serve as a clearinghouse for the problems of the world. The anti-American of the Right resents the United States, above all, for being powerful. He does not find fault with the principle of world domination; but he would like to exercise that domination himself. Moreover, he is afraid of the "corrupting" effect of the American way of life on traditional societies, on societies whose half-rural, half-industrial framework dates back to the nineteenth century. The anti-American of the Left also is upset at the idea of being disturbed. He, too, longs for the nineteenth century—a century at the end of which the "classic" transition from the first industrial revolution to socialism was supposed to take place. It is now evident to him that things have taken a different course; and it is a course that he understands badly, and had never foreseen. Above all, he hates to think that, at the end of the road, a revolution may be waiting—a revolution that is completely new, and that he cannot understand. These two varieties of anti-Americanism, therefore, although they have different motives, share a single function: to explain failure. For the anti-American of the Right, the decline of his own country has been caused by the inordinate increase of American power; that increase has been made possible by the decline of the other great powers. For the anti-American of the Left, the absence, or the failure, of socialist revolutions is what must be explained, and the invention of a foreign scapegoat provides a much needed balm for the ego of the Left which has been so bruised by so many defeats and betrayals. American "imperialism," therefore, is as good an excuse for disappointed socialism as for frustrated nationalism.

One of the most harmful things about anti-Americanism is that it makes it difficult to arrive at factual data. It must therefore be the purpose of analysis to uncover such data concerning contemporary human problems as they are perceived and experienced in America. Whether we are talking about imperialism, freedom, economic struggle, racism, customs, culture, or information, we must try to penetrate to the situation as it really exists in America. And, once we have cleared away the rubble caused by sloth, fear, and absurdity, we most often find enough data to conclude that the situation involves both complexity and conflict.

Certainly, we cannot neutralize anti-Americanism by attempting to replace it with a pro-Americanism that is equally unsophisticated. There has been enough criticism of systematic *anti*-communism, for example, for us to have learned that the hardest thing to cure is systematic *pro*-communism. It is the very concept of any systematic "pro" or "con" position that is so harmful. In my opinion, it is not a matter of either approving or disapproving of American society, but of observing the antagonistic forces at work in that country. To approve or disapprove of a country as a whole is a very primitive way of looking at things. And a senseless one. All that we can try to do is to judge whether or not certain political, economic, and moral realities are leading toward a society which is regarded as a desirable objective. Therefore, it is not my intention to "defend America," because I do not regard America as a single unit. What I would like to do is precisely to show that it is *not* a single unit—so much as that its divisions have brought the country to the verge of civil war.

I maintain that there is a revolutionary America, and an American revolution which is wholly new and which has nothing to do with the revolutions of the nineteenth century—or rather, with the revolutions dreamed of in the nineteenth century. (It is because that revolution is entirely new that Europeans do not recognize it, or are unwilling to recognize it. They feel that, if there is a new revolution and a new civilization, they will have surrendered their own dominant and creative role. Their reaction is one of wounded leftist chauvinism.) If America is indeed in the process of internal conflict, we can conclude that it is probably because there are some things wrong with the system; but we can also conclude that the most important thing, the ability to change, exists in America to a greater extent than in any other country.

JOHAN GALTUNG
A PERILOUS NATION

Johan Galtung is Professor of Peace Research at the University of Oslo, Norway. His conclusion should not startle Americans who are used to reading harsher judgments by native commentators like Anthony Lewis of the New York Times *who claims that "the United States is, today, the most dangerous and destructive power on earth." In Galtung's version there seems to be little hope for the imminent victory of the counter-culture foreseen by Revel.*

This article was first published in the Oslo Newspaper Dagbladet *on May 5, 7, 8, 1973. It was translated by Linda Ricketts Sörbö especially for this volume. Reprinted by permission of Dagbladet.*

The United States is in a state of fundamental crisis, a crisis of confidence more comprehensive than the economic crisis of forty years ago. One after the other the nation's faithful allies like Panama, Venezuela, Canada and Japan are showing signs of strong opposition and neutral countries like Sweden and India are increasingly demonstrating their leanings away from the United States. Kissinger's power game, as elitist as that of Metternich, has brought about some changes in the relationships between the big powers, but only time will show if the relationship with Russia and China is built upon as weak a foundation as the 'peace' in Vietnam. Only time will show how the younger generation in Russia will react when they discover that their parents have sold them into a dependency on Western technology which may prove even stronger than Czarist capitalism. And only time will show if the pictures of Kissinger in Chinese newspapers are a triumph for American or Chinese diplomacy. There are signs that the Chinese are convinced that the United States has not fought its last war in mainland Asia, and that it is in the interest of China to gain time in order to develop those missiles which (perhaps) are necessary to keep the United States from murdering humble Asiatic peasants the rest of this century with the help of increasingly automated warfare.

The Nixon-Kissinger diplomacy led to a coordinated evacuation of POW camps in North Vietnam and troops in South Vietnam. Young men, thin but in a physical condition grotesquely different from the condition of those who creep out of the tiger cages in South Vietnam, returned home and were celebrated as if the return of POWs was the purpose of the war. These defenders of Western privilege were celebrated as heroes in compensation for the victory parade down Fifth Avenue and became the raw material for the mass media industry. I shall never forget one of them I saw on American TV: He had raised a dog in the POW camp and had managed to smuggle it out. For this he was rewarded by an entranced old lady, representing the American Association for the Prevention of Cruelty to Animals, who saw in him the sign of how humane 'our boys' really are. Him, whose mission it was to kill humble Asians! It is difficult, and not even necessary, to refrain from thinking of another friend of dogs, the Auschwitz Commander, Rudolf Höss, or of those B-52 pilots who went on strike because they were not allowed to bring their ice-cream soda to the cockpit.

But there are not many people in the United States who can continue to use the stories of torture from North Vietnam to suppress the nagging doubt which not only includes the war in Indo-China (which continues, as before), but the whole of the United States of America. There is an anxious and agonizing cry for meaning in the U.S. today—for the meaning of the United States and for the meaning of individual lives. It is agonizing because those who cry do not hear any answer other than their own echo. The United States is built on a thesis of almost unlimited individualism, of Darwinistic competition and the belief that the society as a whole functions best when each member is responsible primarily for his own interests. Such a thesis may bring about enormous growth in times of prosperity, but may lead to catastrophe when that prosperity falters.

Americans' fear of the future is a real fear and not an artificial product of an artificial society. Look at the unemployment situation, for example. The American economy is not able to cope effectively with the problem for one very simple reason: Productivity is too high; every employed person produces too much. If production could simply continue to increase this would not be a problem. It may increase as long as new markets are created either spatially, through the world-wide expansion of the American economy, or temporarily, by the constant creation of need for new products, in other words, by planned obsolescence. However, both mechanisms appear to have reached their limits. American products have·an increasingly bad reputation, particularly in the U.S.: Nixon may raise custom duties, but that does not stop people from buying Japanese and German cars. (On the whole, custom duties are much more complicated in their effects than ministries of commerce often seem to think. Higher customs and therefore prices may for example be excellent P.R. [public relations]). Consciousness of planned obsolescence is now so acute that American products are regarded with skepticism precisely for that reason. And so, presumably, they will have to produce more and more through subsidaries in other countries, which will become increasingly independent, and it may well happen that the loyalty is to these companies, wherever they may be, rather than to the 'mother country'.

In the meantime, unemployment will increase in the United States. The employees will, to an increasing extent, be either highly qualified and researchers or abysmally unqualified and receive minimum wages. The relationship between these two groups within a company, for example a car factory in Detroit, will be more and more critical and both groups will be hated by the ordinary workers who will be retired at an earlier age. This situation is very real to those who are layed-off when Boeing reduces production, and they even received packages of food from Seattle's sister city in Japan—an ingenious humiliation. And at the same time, the sympathetic grandson of the Boeing concern goes barefoot and lives in a commune, plays the cello, reads and lives a healthy life, although not really a productive life in an economic sense.

He is symptomatic of the millions of young people who have withdrawn with their soul, if not necessarily with their body. The United States will soon have a disastrous lack of engineers: In 1972, 11% fewer students entered technical schools than in 1971, 18% fewer than in 1970. At the same time, many quit before finishing their studies and the production of engineers is already much lower than what is needed. Investigations reveal that young people do not want an occupation so compromised by warfare and pollution. Moreover, there is a general skepticism towards academic studies, and 'anti-intellectualism' as it is often called by those who do not understand how dehumanized, how blindly positivistic, how 'scientific' American universities have become: Enrollment at the increasingly expensive universities shows a marked decline in the total number of students, while at the same time the economy of the universities is becoming increasingly worse and Nixon's cuts in basic research funds are having their effects.

The war has had an effect on American academic life that reminds one of the Hitler period. Neither hawks nor doves have come up with anything new, the hawks because they no longer believe in what they say themselves, the doves because they do not believe in the value of expressing what they believe. Over a period of years the Left's desire and ability to react has been weakened by a system without any ability to react. Those to whom Nixon refuses to give amnesty, the 68,000 CO's [conscientious objectors], deserters, etc. who are living abroad, largely prefer to remain outside and they may influence university life in Canada in a way similar to the influence exercised by German Jews in the United States 40 years ago. With the growing consciousness in Canada of the 49th parallel as not being a boundary of peace but rather as a boundary between a mother country and her colony, it will soon be apparent once again how short sighted Nixon's politics are. It is almost incredible how minimal the effect of the war has been in American universities. The system continues in spite of the 1968 revolt, and American social scientists, for example, are still largely preoccupied with the same things as they were preoccupied with 15 years ago. This is *not* the case in Europe.

Take the energy crisis as another example. Some gasoline stations are already empty and there is talk of rationing—and not only in Los Angeles. To threaten the potency of the American car must feel like the castration of American self-confidence. The crisis is clear in so far as all curves of demand seem to intersect all curves of supply sometime between now and the year 2000, almost irrespective of whatever is done. The supply may be increased with the help of Alaskan oil, continental shelf oil, increased imports, coal, or nuclear energy, but there are ecological, economic and political difficulties connected with all these solutions. What, for example, would it imply to tap the huge oil reservoirs belonging to the American navy? What would it mean for American 'credibility'? Or, what about the classic solution to use the 6th Fleet of the American Navy in the Mediterranean to occupy one or two oil nations, before the OPEC countries become too obstinate, and before the Ghadfi-Boumedienne policy (we are going to refine the oil ourselves) dominates over the conservative higher-prices-for-raw-oil policy?

The other possibility is to decrease the demand by increasing and improving collective transportation, by lowering the speed limits (lower gasoline consumption) and, above all, by constructing more rational cars. Such measures will probably have disastrous short term effects on American economy which is largely a kind of giant cartel between the automobile and oil industries, with repercussions throughout the entire society. Therefore, the rational solution will, presumably, be as effectively opposed as all the attempts to control the sale of fire arms. Far more probable is a strong increase in gasoline prices (there is talk of 50 cents a gallon). In other words, a rationing which will effect the lower strata of society. And in the meantime everybody hopes that the increasingly smaller number of engineers will find a solution to the problem, while those who would probably be the best engineers have become drop-outs, cop-outs, hippies of various types, critics of society on a full-time basis, or are employed by foreign universities or by foreign companies. Brain-drain from the United States has already become an important factor for the Common Market countries.

How much insight do Americans have into what happens in their own country? There is no lack of information, but on this point the well-known American form of advertising in all mass media must be taken into consideration. We all know that its enormous dimensions make any average American newspaper look like a Christmas catalog from the businessmen in an average Norwegian town, except that it is published daily. The contents of the advertisements are also well known and they are just about as exaggerated and stupid as in Europe. But there is one factor which is more prominent in the United States and which is slightly more fundamental. Advertising in the United States has a fragmenting effect upon every other form of communication: News, weather forecasts, everything is interrupted by advertising which is often broadcast with a slightly higher volume to wake up sleepy news-interested listeners and watchers. In the newspapers, an article is split up in five or six parts in order to force the reader to pursue it through a thicket of ads, to plough through something between one-half to one pound of newspaper until the end of the article is finally reached. That is, if one bothers, if one is not exhausted before one comes that far. On TV and radio it is practically impossible to get any coherent picture out of the news and commentary. The more important and 'hot' a debate is, the more it is interrupted by wealthy companies obviously able to buy themselves into practically anything.

I am not aware of any study on this point, but numerous conversations with Americans make me believe that there is a connection between this fragmentation of every message and the incredibly low level of information concerning foreign policy in the USA. There are powerful moralistic features in the structure of attitudes, and right now the essential feature seems to be that "we are condemned, everything we do is wrong"—but facts are few and far between. It would be a superhuman feat to fit the pieces of the message puzzle, created by ads, back together again, and yet in addition one has to face the fragmentation already created by the press agencies.

Besides, there is less difference between the two newspapers that are published in Honolulu, an average American town, than between *Pravda* and *Izvestia*. They use the same UPI and AP material, some of the same columnists, the same ads and they are printed and edited in the same building, although there is some difference in staffs except for the common Sunday edition. It is of course true that there is a small elite which reads elite newspapers from East and West coast publishers and is excellently informed within their framework of understanding. But an average American will find it just as difficult to obtain decent information on, for example, Cuba or what is happening in the Phillipines, as for a Russian to obtain information on Czechoslovakia. This information must come through foreigners, people who have returned from travels, etc. If any country in the world is in a pre-revolutionary situation, it is the Phillipines, which is also the reason why one hears so little of what happens, so little about American 'advisers', and so little about the feverish drilling of village wells before the communists do it, etc.

Take another main problem, the consumption of pills. After the famous Midtown study in Manhattan revealed that a terribly large number of Americans were in need of psychiatric help (without actually getting it, or even being aware of their situation or its possibilities), attention has been turned towards the general state of mental health. The stereotyped picture of the American as the West Europeans know him—kind, generous, helpful, easy to talk with, well informed —fits poorly with the picture revealed by studying the consumption of pills, pep-pills, sleeping tablets and tranquillizers of all kinds which is, of course, of far greater importance than marijuana, or hash too for that matter. The pharmaceutical companies, however, which inundate the market with such things, are not brought to trial nor is there any threat of maximum punishment: the pills remove some of the symptoms of maladaptation and make the squirrel run in its wheel again: Criticism of the wheel itself and visions of other life forms are not stimulated.

The best schools in the world and the highest number of years in school per inhabitant, and yet so little education. The highest productivity in the world, and yet so little liberation of true creativity. The highest material standard of living, and yet so little well-being. What does all this lead to?

In this connection it is difficult to avoid discussing the enormous violence potential in the United States. I am not thinking so much of the present violent criminality, which, of course, is increasing constantly while theft, etc. shows some decline (Detroit, 1.5 million inhabitants, last year had 601 murders compared to 4 if they had had a Norwegian murder rate). I am thinking more of the violent crimes that may come. It has, for example, been calculated that an 18-year-old average American citizen has watched about 18,000 sadistically performed murders on TV. He has watched TV approximately 3-4 hours a day from the time he was 4 years old, and there is on the average one such murder per hour and all the 'alienated', routine murders, the shoot 'em ups against Indians, etc. are not included in this calculation. There is an increasing number of reports on young murderers who say that 'they wanted to know how it felt to kill someone'. In addition, there are 2.5 million veterans from the Vietnam War returning home from the defeat, and even though the ratio proportion between those who killed and those who assisted those who killed was 1:7, there is a good number who have picked up the trade and lowered their inhibitions against killing off a fellow human being. (This is what the amateur film ''Winter Soldier'' shows with brilliant clarity).

Moreover, there are psychiatric investigations which seem to suggest that the psychological collapse for frustrated veterans will not occur before 5 or 6 years. And added to this is the terribly easy access to arms in the U.S., particularly the so-called 'Saturday Night Special' (a small hand pistol for small murders, ideal for parties or public occasions). It is self-evident that the NRA [National Rifle Association] lobby has been able to oppose effective legislation to sanction gun ownership, and that it is probably too late. There are millions of arms in private hands, nobody knows where, and it would be much easier to hide them than to find them.

There is an increasing frustration and an increasing violence potential and a well established tradition from the sixties to murder political leaders. Then add the latest scandals: Gray in the FBI, Watergate, ITT in Chile. In all of these, sinners will be singled out, displayed and fired to reaffirm the American belief that behind every problem there is a sinner and behind every solution, a hero. Still there are many who, for example, believe in presidential elections, and write articles and books on differences in the personality and 'administrative style' between presidents, without discovering that the American policies in, say, Vietnam survived significant variations on the so-called top level. The FBI will continue more or less as before. After sacrificing a few Nixon people in the White House, the sale of spying equipment will probably increase and lots of Americans will think that 'that guy Nixon was a reasonable fellow who managed to control that communist McGovern'. After some noise over ITT, that case will also be forgotten. That it is a natural career pattern in the United States to go from a position as CIA Director to ITT Director; that American 'advisors' in South Vietnam from now on will be employed by multinational American concerns since they no longer can be paid by the Pentagon; (or a very small thing) that American scientists feel that it is an honor to have their papers printed by the Bobbs-Merrill reprint series, which is also owned by ITT—this will all continue. That is, it will continue as long as ITT's top eschelon finds the USA a worthwhile gamble which is to say it may not last very long.

Add this all up. Frankly speaking, is it probable that a nation which has governed the major part of the world during a short period and is now in the process of collapsing, will quietly collapse like a house of cards? Or, is it more likely that one of the most violent countries in the history of the world will develop progressive and reactionary forms of violence, or, perhaps, both? Imagine American Negroes, Indians (with an average life span of 44 years), Chicanos, women, young unemployed—imagine if they all coordinated their activities and launch Watts, Newark, Detroit, Oglala demonstrations and revolts and strikes all during the same week instead of as now, to distribute all this nicely over time, in order not to overburden Washington? Imagine that this happens at the same time as a delivery strike from energy exporters and continued exchange declines abroad and inflation at home, and one arrives at the same conclusion as the undersigned: The United States today is a perilous country, for itself and for its neighbors.